CeLtic

WOODCRAft

Authentic Projects for Woodworkers

CELTIC

WOODCRAFT

Authentic Projects for Woodworkers

Glenda Bennett

GUILD OF MASTER CRAFTSMAN PUBLICATIONS

Photographic Credits

Anthony Bailey: all finished project photographs.

The Board of Trinity College, Dublin Ireland/Bridgeman Art Library: pp. viii and 27.

By permission of the Parish priest of St Oswald's Church, Ashton-in-Makerfield: pp. 76 and 77.

All other photographs and line drawings supplied by the author.

First published 2002 by
Guild of Master Craftsman Publications Ltd,
166 High Street, Lewes,
East Sussex BN7 1XU

Reprinted 2003

ISBN 1 86108 244 4

British Cataloguing in Publication Data
A catalogue record of this book is available from the British Library.

Design: Fineline Studios

Typefaces: Tiepolo and Aureus Uncial

Colour origination by Viscan Graphics Pte Ltd - Singapore

Printed and bound by Kyodo Printing (Singapore) under the supervision of MRM Graphics, Winslow, Buckinghamshire, UK

Dedication

Dedicated to the memory of my sister, Angela Bennett, who left this world far too soon.

Acknowledgements

My thanks go to the many people who have helped me during the writing of this book: Jimmy and Ernie at Barnes of Barrowford for their invaluable advice and help with tools; Briggs and Duxburys of Barnoldswick for their help with timber, and the parish priest of St Oswald's Church, Ashton-in-Makerfield for kindly allowing me to photograph the stained glass windows.

Special thanks go to David, Daniel, Angela, Kirsten and all my family and friends for their tremendous support and encouragement throughout, and for believing in me.

CONTENTS

The Arrest of Christ, Gospel of St Matthew, Irish (vellum) The Book of Kells, *(c.800.)*

INTRODUCTION

 t Columba, who was born in Ireland around AD520, was possibly one of the most influential people in the history of Celtic art. Following a dispute with the king of Ireland in AD563, over the copyright of a book he had duplicated, St Columba emigrated to Iona, off the west coast of Scotland, to set up the monastery. From there his impact spread throughout Europe, and many of the manuscripts still in existence were produced as a direct result of his influence.

St Columba understood the importance of learning from past masters, not only in an artistic sense, but also in a spiritual way, a lesson that still has relevance today. In his dying prayer for the people of Iona he said:

See that you be at peace among yourselves, my children, and love one another. Follow the example of good men of old.

Much of modern Celtic design is taken from Irish manuscripts of the sixth to eighth centuries, most notably from *The Book of Kells*, the Lindisfarne Gospels and *The Book of Durrow*. But the artists who decorated the gospels contained in these books were drawing on a much older pagan artistic tradition, developed by ancient Celtic tribes. From about 1000BC they occupied a vast area radiating from central Europe to Scotland, Ireland and Spain. Although many different tribes existed and

developed their own cultural diversities, much of Celtic symbolism remained common to them all.

The origins of Celtic art go back as far as 3000BC, when megalithic stone carvings were decorated with geometric patterns, but its full development came between 450BC and 50BC, a time known as La Tène period. The Celts of La Tène period produced bronze repoussé objects for personal wear, as well as for horse ornaments and religious purposes.

From 50BC the Roman Empire grew in strength and influence and consequently much of the Celtic culture was suppressed and diluted, but remote outposts of Western Europe managed to retain their traditions and continued to develop their art. These areas were Galicia in Northern Spain, Brittany, Wales, Scotland, Cornwall, the Isle of Man and Ireland. In Ireland especially, having remained free from Roman control, Celtic art flourished, so by the time Christianity reached there in the fifth and sixth century AD the Celtic artists were able to bring their own unique influences to the illuminated manuscripts that the monasteries produced. Their pagan artistic traditions were not swept aside by the coming of Christianity, but were incorporated into the artwork that decorated the handwritten gospels and enriched them greatly. These insular manuscripts were made up of the four New Testament gospels of Matthew, Mark, Luke and John, written in the Latin of the Vulgate

Figure of a saint in the style of The Book of Kells

Knotwork carved on Pictish stone fragment

translation of the Bible, each gospel being preceded by a canon table.

Although the text of the gospels was the most important element, the pages were lavishly decorated, particularly *The Book of Kells*, of which only two of the 380 folios are without any form of decoration. There are full-page portraits of Christ's life, the evangelists and carpet pages, where every part of the design is filled with intricate knotwork, animals, plants and symbols, as well as over 2,000 decorated letters throughout the book.

It is this distinctive style of decoration from these magnificent manuscripts that is generally recognized as Celtic art, with its two main illustrative styles, geometric and naturalistic. Celtic geometric art features knotwork, spirals and key patterns; naturalistic art features stylized animals, birds, reptiles, plants and humans. I explain the symbolism associated with each motif at the start of the project in which it is introduced.

The Christian monks were representing what was seen as God's work at a time when it was forbidden to copy the work of the Creator. The artist often made mistakes deliberately, to prove his unworthiness.

Depictions of man and beast became very stylised, flat and two-dimensional, and no attempt was made to give perspective to the drawings.

Trying to recreate some of these two-dimensional images as three-dimensional carvings is therefore quite a challenge from a design point of view. Very few examples of woodcarvings from this period survive, partly because of the perishable nature of the material and partly because many wooden votive figures were cast into water as offerings to the deities of the time. The best guides to turning two-dimensional drawings into three-dimensional carvings can be observed from stone carvings, crosses and metalwork.

In 'Further Reading' (page 127) I list several books that contain pictures of

Zoomorphic design on the Aberlemno stone, Scotland

these, if it is not possible to visit the sites of the stones or the museums that contain them.

Geometric patterns are relatively easy to copy in wood, but it is more difficult to retain the apparent simplicity of the anthropomorphic and zoomorphic forms in a three-dimensional carving. To achieve this whilst remaining true to the spirit of Celtic illumination, I have based the projects on low-relief carving techniques.

Even though the 20 projects are diverse in their form and function, the basic techniques remain much the same, which will also make them accessible to those readers with limited woodworking skills.

The projects get progressively more difficult, as each new design element is introduced so, by working through from the first project, the beginner should be able to acquire a good mastery of the subject. For the more advanced carver the projects will hopefully provide a fund of new ideas for an area of Celtic design that has been neglected for too long.

My principal aim in writing this book is to offer Celtic designs for woodworkers, and I hope the fact that I am self-taught will encourage beginners to take up this satisfying craft. The step-by-step instructions show my own method of working, but more experienced woodworkers may want to use their own techniques. To cater for beginners I have, throughout the book, suggested ways in which the projects can be made using the most basic of tools, as well as with the more sophisticated tools that I prefer.

I would strongly advise beginners to check the many excellent reference books available on woodcarving, scrollsaw techniques and tool sharpening, as to attempt to cover these topics would be to move away from the purpose of this book.

Low relief carving of the saint pictured opposite

Above all, whether a beginner or experienced woodcarver, I hope you enjoy the designs and are inspired to design and create your own Celtic pieces.

Note

It is important to read each project through carefully before starting. Measurements are in metric with imperial equivalents in brackets, but please note that conversions may have been rounded to the nearest equivalent. Only one set of measurements should be used, either metric or imperial, and the two must not be mixed.

GETTING STARTED

Tools and Materials

Tools

It is possible to make all the projects in this book with a fairly basic range of tools and, where I have used power tools, I have tried to suggest less expensive hand tools that can be used instead.

Having said that, there is no doubt that power tools can save a lot of time in shape-cutting, and in reducing the bulk of material in certain projects. For the reader who is thinking of investing in new tools, my advice is to buy the best you can afford. I would also recommend taking a training course to acquire power tool skills before making a purchase. Many tool stores run half-day or full-day courses to teach the basics in routing, scrollsawing etc., and these are invaluable for finding out which model would best suit your needs. If it is not possible to attend a course, a lot can be learnt from demonstrators at woodworking exhibitions, who will willingly give free advice and tips on

Basic bench-top scrollsaw

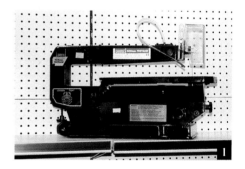

Top-of-the-range scrollsaw

Basic jigsaw and rotary tool with commonly used accessories

their products, so never be afraid to ask. The power tool I use most is a variable speed scrollsaw, but I also use a plunging router, Dremel rotary tool, electric drill and power sander.

On the facing page there is a basic bench-top scrollsaw (1), a top-of-the-range scrollsaw (2), a basic jigsaw that can do a lot of the work of a scrollsaw (but not the fine fretwork), and a rotary tool with some commonly used accessories (3). Where a scrollsaw is not available for making internal cuts, a hand fretsaw with removable blade can be used.

When it comes to woodcarving hand tools, there is a bewildering variety available, but the projects can be made without having to invest in a great range of them. I tend to use my favourite two or three palm tools and a German chip knife in most of my work.

It really is a case of your personal preference when it comes to choosing and using tools. There are many books you can refer to in order to learn more about woodcarving tools, but it is best to work your way systematically through the projects and only acquire new tools as and when you need them. This will not apply, of course, if you already have all the necessary tools and are just looking for new designs to work on.

The most important thing is that, whatever your choice of carving tools, they must always be kept in good condition and sharpened properly.

Materials

There are many timbers suitable for woodcarving in general, but the intricate designs of knotwork are shown at their best when they are made in fine grained and not too highly figured timbers. One of the most suitable is lime, also called basswood, as it has a fine, even grain and, although it is fairly soft to carve, it

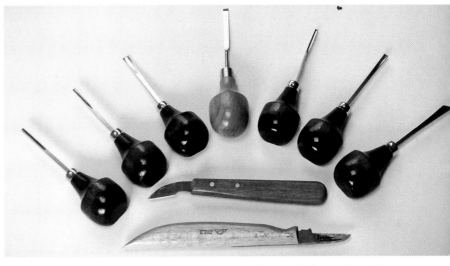

A selection of palm carving tools and chip carving knives

is classed as a hardwood. Sycamore is also a good timber for carving Celtic designs. Both of these woods are very light in colour, so you may prefer to experiment with darker timbers, such as mahogany or cherry, providing the grain patterning is not too pronounced.

Softwoods such as pine may at first seem easy to carve, and can be used for certain applications, but they do not hold detail well and can be easily damaged.

Some of the materials needed to complete the projects

The particular timber that was used in each project is specified in the respective lists of materials.

Various additional materials are used in the projects, many of which can be obtained from good craft stores.

Waxes, varnishes and paints for finishing are all readily available from DIY stores or hardware stores. Other materials, specific to particular projects, can be found as follows:

Project 3, Initial Memo Holder (page 18): Crocodile clips and wire can be bought from audio or auto stores. Alternatively, copper wire can be obtained very cheaply by stripping the plastic covering from electrical cable.

Project 9, Hand Mirror (page 37): Small round mirrors can be purchased from craft stores or woodturning supplies stores.

Project 10, Dragon Trinket Box (page 41): Brass can usually be obtained from sheet metal merchants, or it may be possible to obtain it from shops that supply trophies and engraved plaques.

Project 14, Mirrored Candle Sconce (page 57): Christmas tree candles and holders are usually available from craft stores but, if not, they can be bought by mail order from craft suppliers or department stores. A list of mail order craft suppliers can be found in craft magazines. Small square and round mirrors can be purchased from craft stores.

Project 16, Coasters in Holder (page 64): Veneers can be obtained from specialist timber suppliers, as well as some good craft stores.

Project 18, Claddagh Mirror (page 71): DIY stores or woodturning supplies stores usually stock round mirrors.

Project 19, Stained Glass Uplighter (page 76): Acrylic sheet is available at DIY stores, along with self-adhesive lead and the light fitting. Art and craft stores stock glass paints and imitation lead outliner.

Workshop safety

Working with wood can be immensely satisfying and a finished piece can give a great sense of pride and achievement, but nothing can be accomplished without the use of tools. Even using the simplest knife for whittling immediately creates the need for an awareness of safety rules.

Most safety advice is a matter of common sense, but there is nothing wrong with a timely reminder to take care. You will, after all, get far more pleasure from producing beautiful woodcraft if your hands are not covered in bandaids at the end.

Treating your tools and machines with respect and caution will reduce the risk of accidents, and the following advice is given for the purpose of minimizing mishaps, but please remember: your personal safety is your own responsibility.

Safety tips

• Be in the right frame of mind: tiredness, carelessness or irritability can lead to poor judgement, which not only increases the potential for mistakes and mishaps, it can also lead to frustration and disappointing results.

• Never operate tools whilst under the influence of alcohol or medication that causes drowsiness.

• Always wear appropriate safety wear. Safety goggles, dust mask and ear defenders should be worn whenever power tools are being used: the dust produced when working with wood can cause irritation to the skin, eyes and respiratory system, as well as the possibility of fungal infections. MDF dust contains resins which are used in the manufacturing process, and this dust should not be inhaled, so masks must be worn when working with both MDF and wood.

• Loose clothing is not suitable when using power tools, and long hair should be tied back. Be aware of the potential risk that jewellery may present.

• Secure your work with clamps or a vice whenever possible so that both hands are free to steady the tool being used. The step-by-step photographs in the projects tend not to include clamps in order to show the procedure more clearly, and occasionally pieces can be too small to clamp practically, but try to get into the habit of securing work wherever possible.

• Always keep fingers behind the blade on hand tools. If you have to hold a work piece, always cut away from the hand that is doing the holding.

• Keep your work area free from clutter, and use good lighting.

• Always switch off and disconnect power tools when changing accessories or blades, or when servicing.

• Never operate power tools in wet or damp conditions.

• Always follow the manufacturer's instructions for the tool being used, and take heed of the additional safety advice specific to each type of tool.

• The most important safety advice of all is to always keep cutting edges sharp. Dull edges can slip on wood, but will not slip on skin.

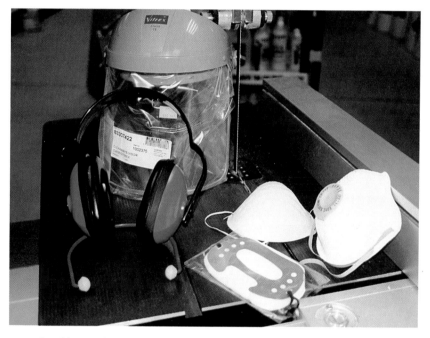

Examples of face masks and ear defenders for protection when using power tools

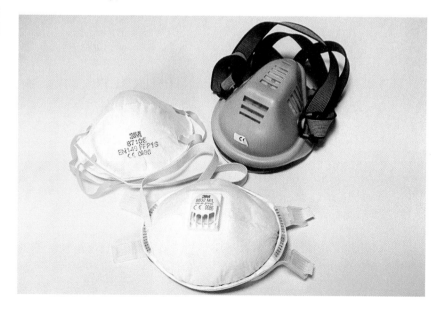

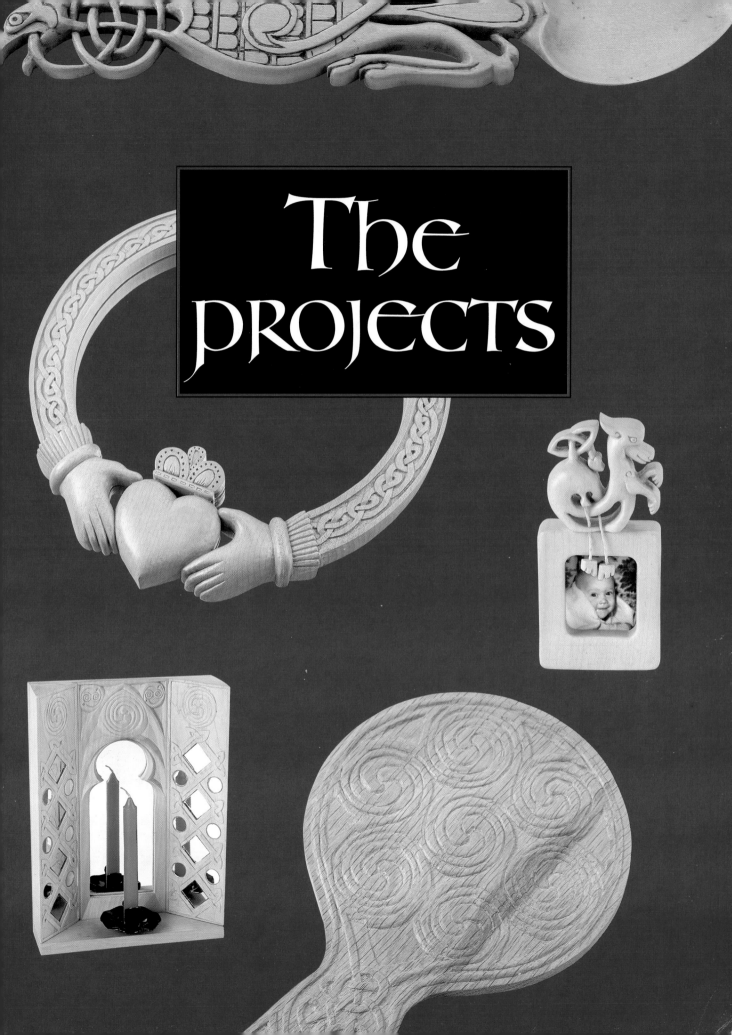

The PROJECTS

Celtic knotwork border

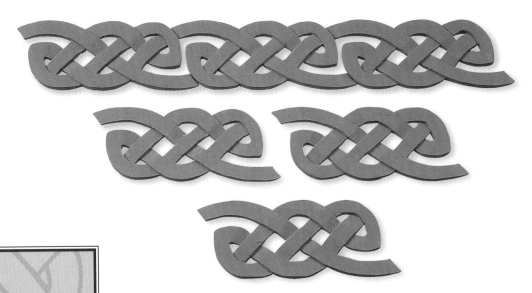

Materials

Several photocopies of template 1A (see page 87), enlarged by 125%

Pine strip wood, 6 x 68mm (¼ x 2¾in) x length required

Repositionable spray adhesive

Double-sided sticky tape

Paint, varnish or wax finish, as required

Tools

Scrollsaw, electric jigsaw or hand fretsaw

Drill fitted with small bit

12mm (½in) straight chisel

Craft knife or chip knife

This project shows you how to achieve the ribbon-like interlacing so typical of Celtic knotwork, which forms the basis of many of the designs in this book. The simple but impressive border adds the perfect finishing touch to a room and, by using a variety of finishes, you can achieve a highly individual look.

Celtic knotwork, which appears on stone crosses of the sixth century AD and onwards, and in the intricate pattern-filling designs of the eighth-century illuminated manuscripts, can be made up of one, two or more interlacing bands. Some people believe that there is no symbolism attached to the different types of knotwork, and it is probable that meaning has been conferred in more recent times. It is easy to see, however, why other people believe that the unbroken bands of the knotwork represent a sacred path through life, with no beginning or end, an eternal journey of spiritual growth.

This project may look daunting but, because the design is worked in small manageable sections, it is not difficult to make. The main skill required is patience, and in my experience you wouldn't be a woodworker if you did not already possess this trait.

Once the sections are complete, they join to make a continuous border, as shown, which can be cut to fit corners. Alternatively, if you want to use the border to decorate small pieces of furniture, cupboards or boxes, simply reduce the design to the size required.

Method

1 Cut the strip wood into 200mm (8in) lengths and make a stack of four as shown, using double-sided sticky tape to hold them firmly together. (If you already have experience of stack cutting, you may find you can cope with more than four.)

2 Stick template 1A on the top of the stack – use spray adhesive, as this will make it easy to remove after cutting.

3 Drill a hole in each of the shaded areas of the template, to allow access to make the internal cuts.

4 Cut out the internal shaded areas, threading the blade through the drilled hole first. A scrollsaw is ideal for this, but if you don't have access to one, a hand fretsaw or an electric jigsaw fitted with a narrow scrolling blade will do the job.

5 Finally cut round the outside of the design, carefully separating the pieces and removing all traces of sticky tape.

6 Using the original template as a guide, transfer all the crossing lines onto the pieces with a light pencil mark. It is essential to copy the lines faithfully so that the woven effect is even and continuous, especially when pieces are joined end to end.

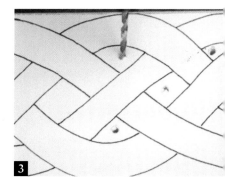

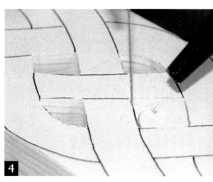

7 With a sharp chip knife or craft knife, score along these lines to a depth of 3mm (⅛in).

8 Using the chisel at right angles to each line, gradually slope the wood down towards the line, so that the band appears to weave under and over, as shown. Also reduce the wood by 3mm (⅛in) at each end of the border where it will meet the next piece.

9 Give each piece a final light sanding.

To complete the project, you have a choice of finishes:

- Varnish the border, then fix it in place around the wall using a suitable adhesive such as 'No More Nails'.

- Alternatively, if you wish the border to contrast with its background, prime and paint the sections first, then glue in place as above.

- To give the effect of a plaster relief finish, prime the wood before sticking it in place, then paint the whole wall and Celtic border with the same paint.

- Or, to achieve the antique weathered-bronze effect, apply a base coat of emulsion paint in a terracotta colour after priming. When dry apply a coat of metallic copper paint. Allow to dry and then dip a small stencil brush in gold metal paint, wipe off until almost dry, and then stipple randomly over the copper. Repeat with another darker shade of copper until the desired effect is achieved (see below).

The antique, weathered-bronze effect

Knotwork overlays

he previous knotwork border is just one example of the variety of Celtic knotwork designs that exist. Single knotwork motifs can be used to great effect as overlays on a variety of objects, and are made using similar techniques to the previous project.

Four different templates for overlays are provided on page 88 but, once they have been mastered you will be able to use other patterns from Celtic art source books to make your own overlays.

The templates can be enlarged to any size to suit the object they are to decorate, and I suggest enlarging by 140% for the first attempts, as this will make the internal cuts easier.

Some suggested uses for the overlays:

• Decorate the lid of a purchased or home-made box (above left).
• Use four matching corners to decorate a chunky plain picture frame (right).
• Decorate drawer-fronts or doors on furniture.
• Make the same design in contrasting timbers to create a semi-abstract picture.
• Connect the open-ended pattern (template 2A, on page 88) with straight strips of matching timber to form a frame, as shown in the drawing overleaf.

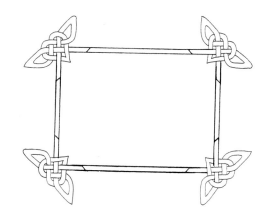

Materials

Enlarged photocopy of template 2A, 2B, 2C or 2D (as preferred: see page 88)

Assorted timbers to size of template (or enlargement), 4–6mm (^{5}/$_{32}$–^{1}/$_4$in) thick (e.g. pink ivory, jarra, American hard maple, hardwood strip)

Repositionable spray adhesive

Double-sided sticky tape

Glue

Clear wax polish, varnish, or preferred finish

Tools

Scrollsaw or hand fretsaw

Small chisel

Chip knife or craft knife

Drill with small drill bit

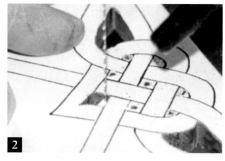

Method

1 Place the chosen template onto the smooth face of timber using spray adhesive. Drill pilot holes in all the areas to be cut out.

2 Using a scrollsaw or hand fretsaw, thread the blade through the pilot holes and make the internal cuts. Make sure the corners have sharp angles, with no roundedness.

3 Cut round the outside of the design.

4 Remove the template and transfer all the lines of the knotwork onto the face of the timber, using the template as a guide to which way they cross. It is important to get the lines right at this stage so that the weaving effect will be correctly carved.

5 Score along the lines using a sharp knife.

6 Use the chisel at right angles to the line and lower the material on either side of a crossing band, to give the appearance of weaving underneath. Slope it down to about half the depth of the timber. The angle of the slope will depend on how closely the bands are to each other – some will need to be quite steep to achieve the depth, while others can be more gradual.

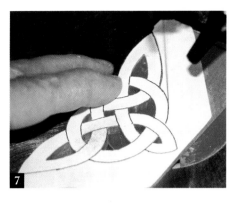

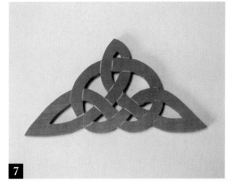

7

7

7 The photographs above show a different, enlarged, template (2B) being used on a piece of 'pink ivory' variety of timber, which was used to decorate the box lid on page 15.

8 If you wish to make a set of four corners, use the same stack-cutting technique as in the previous project (see page 13). Cut four pieces of timber to the approximate size of the template and layer firmly together using double-sided tape. Stick the template on top using spray-mount adhesive.

9 Drill pilot holes through all four layers.

10 Cut out the waste areas.

11 Cut round the outside of the design.

12 Carefully separate the pieces and clean off any glue residue. Transfer the lines onto the face of each piece.

13 Score along the lines with a sharp knife.

14 Lower the material on each side of the crossing band to create the weaving effect.

15 Seal the overlays using clear wax polish, varnish, paint or any other chosen finish, before gluing to your chosen object.

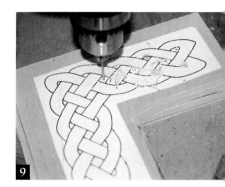

9

11

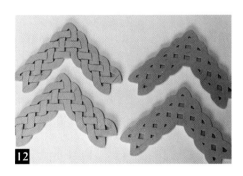

12

14

Initial memo holder

Materials

Photocopies of letter templates 3A–3E, as required (see pages 89–93), enlarged by 125%

For each initial, a piece of timber approx. 80 x 110 x 25mm (3¼ x 4½ x 1in) (Some letters may require wider or narrower timber)

Piece of wire 70mm (2¾in) long, 2mm (³⁄₃₂in) diameter

Small crocodile clip

Glue

Repositionable spray adhesive

Tools

Scrollsaw or fretsaw

Drill with 2mm (³⁄₃₂in) bit

Pliers

Small chisel

Chip carving knife or craft knife

The previous two projects have demonstrated the method of carving knotwork in a fretwork style. This project shows you how to carve knotwork in low relief, that is, onto the surface of the timber. This technique will be employed in many of the projects that follow.

Initial letters were used to decorate the manuscripts produced by Celtic artists, and range in design from simple black letters to the most elaborate and ornate letters imaginable. Indeed some are so elaborate that it can be difficult for the untrained eye to decipher them. In manuscripts such as *The Book of Kells* this was almost irrelevant, since the artist could indulge in stunning flights of fantasy when decorating letters, sure in the knowledge that the scholarly reader would be very familiar with the text.

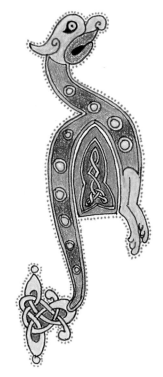

Initial letter A in the style of The Book of Kells

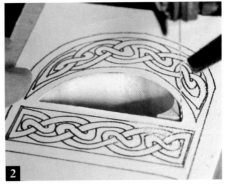

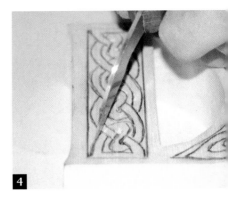

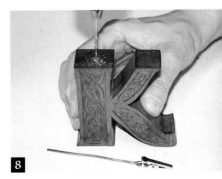

Ornate capitals enabled the reader to locate a particular passage in the text and the initial letters carved here have been given a purpose of their own – by adding a simple wire and crocodile clip they serve as a memo or photograph holder. The clip is strong enough to hold a small photo, business card, shopping reminder or message. Or they could, if preferred, be used purely as decorative objects without the wire and clip.

Method

1 Photocopy the chosen letter and stick it to the timber with spray adhesive. If necessary, drill a pilot hole for blade access to cut out the centre of the letter.

2 Use a scrollsaw or fretsaw to cut out the letter.

3 To transfer the design to the wood, place carbon paper between the template and the wood and trace round the design.

4 Score carefully along the outside lines of the design using a sharp chip knife or craft knife.

5 Carefully lower the background around the knotwork to a depth of 1–2mm ($\frac{1}{16}$–$\frac{3}{32}$in).

6 Score the crossing lines of the knotwork to half the depth of the raised bands using a sharp knife. Slope bands down at right angles to the lines on either side of the crossing points, as in the previous project (see page 16 step 6).

7 To assemble the clip holder, fasten the crocodile clip around one end of the piece of wire, using the pliers to achieve a very tight fit. Make sure that the clip cannot move around on the wire, using a dab of glue if necessary.

8 Drill a hole in the top of the letter using the 2mm ($\frac{3}{32}$in) drill bit. (If your piece of wire is of a different diameter, use a drill bit that corresponds to it.)

9 Place the plain end of the wire in the drilled hole, using a small amount of glue to hold it in place if necessary.

10 Seal the wood with wax or varnish as preferred.

Claddagh Lovespoon

he tradition of giving lovespoons is alleged to have originated in Wales during the seventeenth century, when a young man would carve a piece of wood into a spoon to give to his love as a token of courtship. It is possible that the degree of intricacy in the carving reflected the greatness of his love.

Lovespoon designs often incorporate Celtic knotwork along the handle, and I have developed this idea further by adapting the traditional Claddagh design from Galway. Claddagh is a small village on the coast of Galway Bay in Ireland, and the distinctive Claddagh design is said to have been developed by a native of the village, Richard Joyce, who fashioned gold rings.

The heart, hands and crown represent love, friendship and loyalty. The legend is that when the Claddagh ring is worn on the right hand with the heart pointing outwards, it shows that the wearer is unattached, with a free heart. If the heart points inwards a love is being considered. Worn on the left hand with the heart pointing inwards means two loves have become inseparable.

There are many suitable timbers that can be used to make the lovespoon – here I have used American tulipwood, which is fairly easy to carve with the most basic of tools. You can see from the photographs that good results can be achieved using even the least expensive of craft knifes. As always though, use the tools that you are most comfortable with and, most importantly, always keep a good sharp edge.

Method

1 Prepare a good smooth surface on the back and front on your timber: use a plane if it is very uneven, then sand with medium (120 grade) to fine (180 grade) sandpaper. Fix the template to the front of the timber using spray adhesive.

2 Drill a pilot hole in each of the shaded areas to allow access for the fretsaw/scrollsaw blade.

3 Make all the internal cuts first, by threading the fretsaw/scrollsaw blade through the pilot hole, then cutting round the internal lines.

4 When all the internal cuts are complete, cut around the outside of the lovespoon. Remove the template and transfer the guidelines onto the wood as shown.

5 Starting with the central 'handle' section, use a sharp chip knife, craft knife, or chisel to score along the lines where the bands will cross over and under. It is essential to keep these in the right order so the weaving works correctly. Score to a depth of about 2mm (³⁄₃₂in) to begin with, then using a straight chisel at right angles to each line, gradually reduce the wood at each side of the weave.

6 Next round over the edges of the bands using a knife or chisel, taking care to also round the corners where the band appears to cross under another. Round off the bands all the way round the top and down as far as the point where they meet the cuffs above the hands, then reduce the area behind the cuffs by a millimetre or two to make the cuffs more prominent.

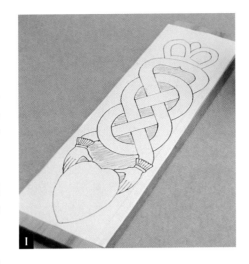

1

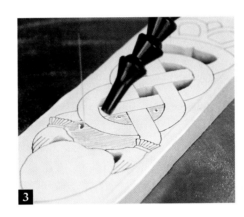

3

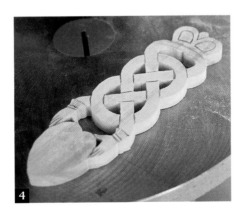

4

5

Materials

Tracing or photocopy of template 4A (see page 94), enlarged by 111%

Piece of timber, 230 x 70 x 12mm (9 x 2¾ x ½in) (American tulipwood)

Repositionable spray adhesive

Wax or other preferred finish

Tools

Plane (optional, if the timber is very uneven)

Sandpaper, if required

Scrollsaw, jigsaw fitted with scrolling blade or hand fretsaw

Drill fitted with small wood bit

Chip knife or craft knife

12mm (½in) chisel

Rotary tool (optional) or gouge for bowl shaping

Round punch and hammer

7 Shape the back of the spoon into a convex shape, tapering the pointed end more steeply towards the front. (If you need help with the shape, use the shape of a spoon from the cutlery drawer as a guide.) I used a tungsten burr bit fitted on the Dremel to remove the bulk of the waste, followed by a sanding drum, but you could use a gouge to shape the back instead.

8 Scoop out the inside bowl of the spoon, carefully checking the depth as you go along and matching the shaping you have given the back: aim to achieve an even thickness over the whole of the bowl of the spoon. Again I used the Dremel for this, but a gouge can be used if preferred.

9 Round over the sides of the cuffs and hands, then taper the ends of the fingers and thumbs down, so that they appear to be holding the heart from just behind. Next, score along each side of the bands at the wrists, taper down the wood on both sides of these, then round over the edges of the band as shown. Re-mark the guidelines for the frills on the cuffs and the fingers.

10 Use a V-tool, if you have one, to make the lines between the cuffs and fingers, otherwise a craft knife or chip knife can be used. Round over all the sections of the cuffs and the fingers.

11 Now shape the crown. First reduce the depth by about 2mm (³⁄₃₂in) and use a chisel to bevel it down where it meets the top band. Notch the 'V' of the little triangular shape at the top, then curve just this part.

12 Using a punch about 4mm (⁵⁄₃₂in) in diameter, make a series of circle shapes all round the outside and down the middle. I improvised as you can see, by taking a ball pen to pieces and using the metal ferrule as a punch. Fortunately it survived the experience and lived to write another day.

13 Mark a line around the inner edge of the punched circles, then score it with a sharp knife or V-tool. Cutting from inside this line, angle the blade and cut away some of the wood to give the appearance of puffy material. Create some creases at the bottom using either a V-tool or knife.

14 Sand if necessary, then apply a coat of wax (or your preferred finish). I find an old, soft toothbrush ideal for this, as it can get into most of the nooks and crannies of the carving. When dry, buff with a lint-free cloth.

15 To hang the lovespoon, drill a small hole in the back of the crown. A small nail or tack in the wall is all that is necessary to hook it onto.

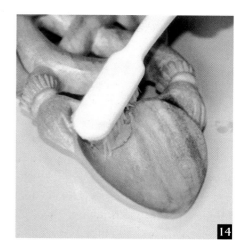

Double photo frame

his project introduces the Celtic zoomorphic motif in an elementary form, combined with the style of knotwork used for the Initial Memo Holder (page 18). The serpentine body of a dog forms the borders of the frame, with its head and tail completing the design. The ear lappet extends to form the knotwork on one side, with the tail dividing to make the knotwork on the opposing side. As is common in zoomorphic design, the tongue also gives rise to a little flourish of its own. Normally a dog design would have at least two legs visible, but I wanted to keep the outline of the frame fairly simple, so this hapless creature will have to remain a victim of artistic licence.

There was great belief among the Celts that their deities were capable of shape-shifting or metamorphosis, taking on the guise of animals and birds. This gave rise to the many zoomorphic forms to be seen in the earliest Celtic art. A panel on the first century BC Gundestrup Cauldron depicts the forest god Cerunnos with antlers on his head and holding a snake that has ram's horns. Both the antlers and snakeskin are symbolic of regeneration, as they can be shed and re-grown. Numerous other examples of zoomorphic design appear in manuscripts such as *The Book of Kells* and the *Lindisfarne Gospels*, and the magnificent Ardagh Chalice and Cross of Cong, housed in the National Museum of

Ireland, Dublin, have many exquisitely crafted filigree panels of interlaced birds and beasts.

Animals were revered by the Celts and symbolized the power of nature, yet were often compared to humans in terms of their qualities of loyalty and bravery. It is this melding of human and animal qualities that makes the zoomorphic designs so fascinating.

I have deliberately used 25mm (1in) deep timber to make the frame, so that it will be freestanding when finished. If you would prefer it to be less chunky, then by all means use thinner stock and make the rebate shallower, then make either a supporting stand for the back, or attach a hanger to the back for wall hanging.

Method

1 Ensure that the face and back of the timber are perfectly even and smooth, planing if necessary, then sanding with medium or fine sandpaper. Stick the template to the face side of the timber, using spray adhesive.

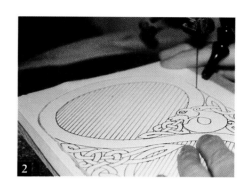

2 Cut round the outside of the design on the scrollsaw or, if you prefer hand tools, use a fretsaw.

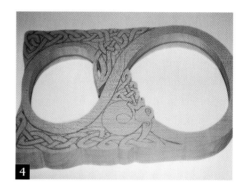

3 Drill a pilot hole in each of the three shaded areas to accept the scrollsaw or fretsaw blade, then cut out these internal areas.

4 Carefully lift off the template and remove any glue residue from the face of the timber by sanding with fine sandpaper. Replace the template on the wood, slip some carbon paper beneath it and place a little masking tape at the side to hold the template in place. Trace the knotwork design onto the surface of the wood.

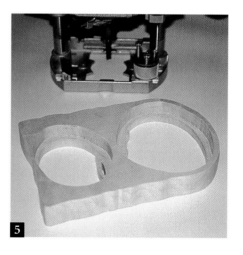

5 Before starting to carve, turn the frame over and make the rebates for the photographs: mark a line approximately 4mm (^{5}⁄$_{32}$in) in from the cutouts and then make a rebate with the router to a depth of 12–15mm (^{1}⁄$_2$–^{5}⁄$_8$in). (If you do not have access to a router, the rebates can be made using a chisel.) You will need to make several passes with the router, about 3mm (^{1}⁄$_8$in) deep each successive time, to avoid putting excessive pressure on the cutting bit.

6 To make the backing pieces that hold the photographs in place, lay the frame face side up on the 4mm (^{5}⁄$_{32}$in) board and draw a line round the inside of the rebate onto the board as shown. Cut these two pieces out using a scrollsaw or fretsaw.

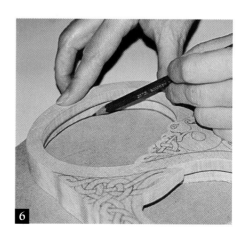

7 Next, turn the frame face upwards, and score along the lines of the knotwork using a chip knife, craft knife or chisel.

8 Using the chisels and gouges, remove the material between the bands of knotwork, aiming to cut the background to a depth of 2–3mm ($^3/_{32}$–$^1/_8$in) to allow for definition. Some of the small areas to be removed are best tackled with the point of a chip knife, or a scalpel can be used on softer timbers.

9 When all the background has been lowered, begin to make the weaving effect of the bands. Make sure that the crossing lines have been scored, then lower the material on either side of each crossing point using a straight chisel, working at right angles to each band. Where a band crosses another in close proximity, the gradient of the cut must be fairly steep, but can be more gradual where the crossing point is further away from the next.

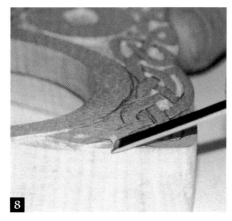

10 Where each of the bands comes to an end, form it into a ball shape.

11 Reduce the depth of the body on either side of the head by about 1–2mm ($^1/_{16}$–$^3/_{32}$in) to enable the head to be carved. Round off the top of the head and reduce the level of the material around the jaw line and up to the ear lappet. Round the edges of the cheek, jaw and snout and give definition to the tongue and teeth. Make a groove for the nostril with a knife or V-tool.

12 Shape the eye by marking out the lines with a sharp knife. Remove the triangular shape behind the eyeball

then round the sides of the eyeball by cutting the scored lines down at an angle. Mark out the small circle at the centre of the eye.

13 Complete the frame by carefully sanding where necessary, then apply at least two coats of clear wax polish, or a finish of your choice.

14 Cut your photos to size using the backing pieces as a template. If you wish to make a protective front for the photograph, cut a piece of acetate the same size. Put the acetate and photograph in the frame, with the backing pieces behind, and hold it all in place with small tacks or glaziers' points.

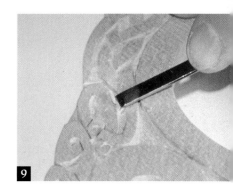

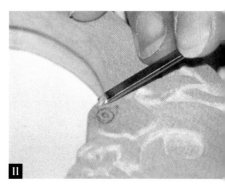

Eagle wall plaque

Materials

Photocopy of template 6A
(see page 96), enlarged to
176%

Timber measuring
390 x 165 x 25mm
(15¼ x 6½ x 1in) (lime)

Repositionable spray
adhesive

Clear wax or preferred
finish

Tools

Scrollsaw or fretsaw

Chisels and gouges

Rotary tool (optional)

Craft knife or chip knife

The eagle is associated with strength and wisdom. It appears many times in illuminated manuscripts as an evangelist symbol for St John, although in *The Book of Durrow* the eagle is used to represent St Mark. In Durrow, the eagle is very stylized, having a perfectly round head and eye facing right, with a forward facing body.

In *The Book of Kells* the eagle appears much more frequently, giving the opportunity for a far greater variety of designs. Some eagles are depicted with four wings, and one has even been given a hand with which to hold a book.

Along with the three other evangelist symbols, lion, calf and man, the symbols were taken as a reference to Christ's incarnation, the soaring eagle representing the Ascension.

Eagle in the style of The Book of Kells

Eagle in the style of The Book of Durrow

Folio v from The Book of Kells

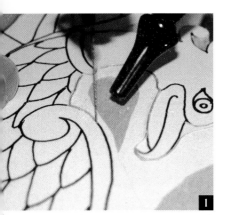

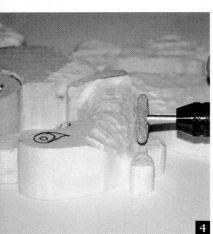

Method

1 Paste the enlarged template onto the timber and cut round the outside using a scrollsaw or hand fretsaw. Take particular care around the head and feet and make sure the corner cuts are nice and sharp.

2 Transfer the lines of the design onto the timber, but don't transfer all the chest feather details at this stage, as they would disappear during the initial shaping.

3 Begin roughing out the shape of the eagle, reducing the depth of the front leg by about half and the back leg by about a third. Reduce the depth of the left-hand wing by about a third, working around the neck-ring. To save time I reduced most of the bulk using a structured tungsten carbide bit in my Dremel, but it could also be carved with chisels and gouges.

4 To allow the neck-ring to sit proud, reduce either side by 2mm ($\frac{3}{32}$in), and then round over the sides of the neck and head. Reduce the two head feathers at the same time by about 6mm ($\frac{1}{4}$in).

5 Reduce the beak by about 6mm ($\frac{1}{4}$in) as you round off the front of the head.

6 Round over the edges of the chest, back and body down towards the legs. Round the legs and taper in the ankles.

7 Take about 2–3mm ($\frac{3}{32}$–$\frac{1}{8}$in) off the depth of the whole right-hand wing, below the topmost feather and large curl.

8 Keeping the overall depth uniform, round over the top and bottom edges of the neck-ring and curve it around the neck.

9 Once all this basic shaping has been achieved, add the finer details. First step down the wing feathers from the top row, nearest the body, to the wing tip. To achieve this, pencil in the lines for the top row of feathers, then score around them with a sharp chip knife or craft knife. Create the step-down effect by reducing all the material behind the lines to a depth of 2mm ($\frac{3}{32}$in), working in the direction of the wing tip. Once the first row of feathers is complete, mark out the next row, repeating the process and stepping down each time by about 2mm ($\frac{3}{32}$in).

10 Work the long lateral feathers in a similar way, stepping them down from top to bottom lengthwise.

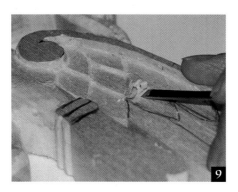

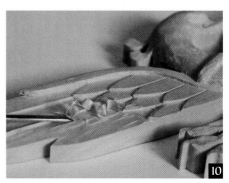

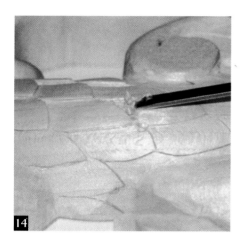

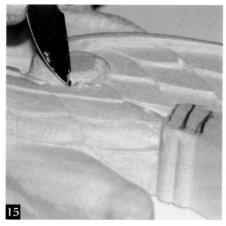

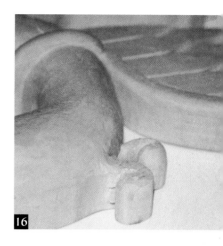

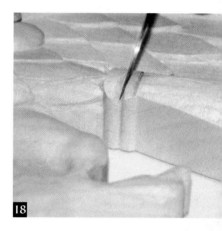

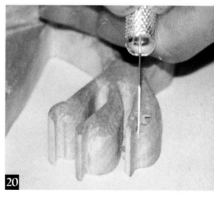

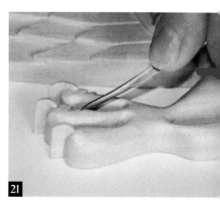

11 When all the long feathers have been stepped down you will notice that the previously carved feathers have been left with irregular depths, and these can now be sloped down towards the bottom of the wing to regain uniform depth.

12 Round over the top feather that runs the length of the wing, reducing the tip as necessary to give an even depth.

13 Smooth the chest of the eagle and taper the body where it meets the ring of tail feathers by about 5mm (³⁄₁₆in). Round it over into the back at the same time.

14 Draw in the feathers on the chest and then score along the lines. Working from the neck end towards the tail, define each feather by lowering the adjacent feather where it meets, but keep the tip of the next feather at its original height.

Make sure that the original shape of the body is maintained while these feathers are being carved.

15 Round over the edges of the large curl at the front of the right wing, to make it into a dome shape.

16 Round the two feathers at the back of the head, making the terminal into a ball shape as shown.

17 Reduce the depth of the tail feathers, behind the two rings, by about 5mm (³⁄₁₆in) as for the body, and then round over the sides.

18 Mark the line in the middle of the ring, notch a 'V' along this line and round over the sides of the rings. Also shape the rings around the body, keeping the depth uniform.

19 Mark in the two lines along the length of the tail feathers and notch a 'V' into them, widening the 'V' towards the tip of the feathers. Round over the side edges of each feather as before.

20 Round over the sides of the legs and toes but leave the claws as high as possible to allow for shaping. Make each claw appear to grow out of its cuticle, by notching into the base of the claw to create a crease.

21 Taper the tip of the claw downwards and round along its length. Next, make two creases behind each cuticle by marking out with a curved gouge and then undercutting behind the curve.

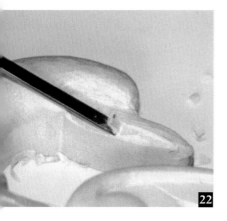

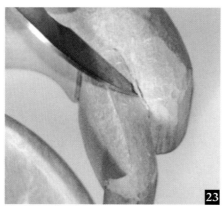

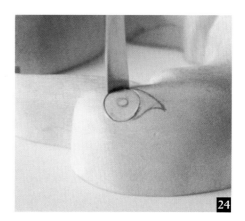

22 To finish the head, reduce the lower half of the beak by scoring along the mid-line and paring away about 2mm (³⁄₃₂in).

Round over the top and lower edges of the beak.

23 Undercut the point where the forehead and cheek meet the beak to give greater definition.

24 Pencil in the eye, then use a gouge with the same sweep of curve to mark it out, keeping the tool at right angles to the head.

25 Shape the eye by chamfering into the marked line with a sharp knife, leaving the centre of the eye dome-shaped.

Mark the small circle in the centre of the eye with the tip of a knife.

26 The diagonal lines along the wing feathers are made by cutting down at right angles with a straight chisel, or by using a V-tool to mark along the line.

27 If necessary, sand lightly, and then apply the finish of your choice. I used a clear wax polish and then, to give the appearance of age, I went over it with a dark wax polish. I wiped this off before it dried, so that it stayed in the lines and creases, then applied a further coat of clear wax polish.

28 To allow the eagle to be hung on a wall, drill a 2mm (³⁄₃₂in) hole in the back, slightly off-centre to counterbalance the difference in size and shape of the wings. This can then be hooked over a small nail tapped into the wall, so that it sits flush against the wall.

ꟿessage board

 he border on this message board introduces a new style of knotwork. Instead of the open-weave knotwork of the previous projects, here it is closely intertwined so that no spaces are visible between the bands. It is still possible to trace the path of each band that makes up each eternal knot, but it requires just a little more concentration.

Concentration is also the key to successful carving in this project, in order to maintain the correct weaves of the bands but, once you master the technique, the effect is very pleasing.

The message board itself is a blackboard for good old-fashioned chalk, which can be cleaned and re-written, but alternative surfaces could be used such as a cork board, used with pushpins, or a whiteboard that can be used with dry-wipe marker pens.

The wording at the top of the board can easily be changed for something that has a personal meaning; it doesn't necessarily have to be a place, as I have chosen. A single word works best, however, so that the letters can be joined and cut out as one. If nothing inspires you, you could do worse than choosing just the word 'messages'.

Materials

Photocopy of template 7A, enlarged to 188% (see page 97) and 7B, C or D, if desired (see page 98)

Piece of timber measuring 400 x 290 x 12mm (15¾ x 11½ x ½in) (lime)

Piece of MDF measuring 400 x 290 x 4mm (15¾ x 11½ x 5⁄32in)

Repositionable spray adhesive

Carbon paper

Wood glue

Varnish

Primer

Blackboard paint

Tools

Scrollsaw or fretsaw

Drill

Router (if available)

Selection of chisels and gouges

Chip knife or craft knife

After much deliberation, I chose 'Glastonbury' as my header. Glastonbury in Somerset, England, is a mystical and enigmatic place, and the Tor that rises from the surrounding plains has given rise to many myths and legends.

The early Celts regarded high ground as a sacred place, and revered it as such. The Celts saw their gods as the personification of the natural forces around which their lives revolved.

The Tor itself was believed to be magically hollow, with a secret entrance to the Isle of Avalon hidden in its side. Avalon was the realm of King Arthur who, in the sixth century, defended the Celts against the Anglo-Saxon invasions, following the withdrawal of the Romans.

Endless myths and legends have grown up around King Arthur and his Knights of the Round Table, and many places lay claim to being the site of his court, including Cornwall and Wales. The truth is that as a great king he would have had many strongholds up and down the country, Glastonbury Tor being but one, albeit a significant one. His famous magician, Merlin, was credited with laying out a huge ten-mile wide zodiac around the Tor, using features in the landscape.

The Tor is also reputed to be the burial place of the Holy Grail: after the crucifixion, Saint Joseph of Arimathea is said to have brought the chalice used in the Last Supper to Glastonbury, and buried it on the Tor at Chalice Well.

Whatever one chooses to believe, there is no doubting the importance of Glastonbury in folklore, and in the continuing fascination with its mystical associations.

Method

1 Stick photocopied template 7A onto the face of the timber, using spray adhesive. Cut around the outside with a scrollsaw or fretsaw.

2 Drill a pilot hole in the central waste area to allow the blade to pass through. Cut out the internal waste, carefully following the curves of the design.

3 Transfer the design onto the face of the framework, using tracing paper.

4 On the reverse, mark a straight line 5mm ($^3/_{16}$in) away from the cut out section. Use this as a guide to make a 4mm ($^5/_{32}$in) deep rebate.

If you want to make pierced lettering rather than raised lettering, make the rebated area reach within 5mm ($^3/_{16}$in) of the top of the frame, following the arched shape. You can then cut letters out so that the black of the backing board shows through (see step 12). If possible, use a router to cut the rebate – otherwise use a chisel, and square off the bottom corners using a small chisel.

5 Cut out a piece of the 4mm ($^5/_{32}$in) thick MDF, to fit in the routed area. The easiest way to get an accurate fit is to lay a sheet of tracing paper on the board, trace the routed shape, then use it as a template. When cut out it will be used to make the chalk board, but it can be put to one side for now.

6 Score along the lines of the design on the face of the frame, using a sharp chip knife or craft knife.

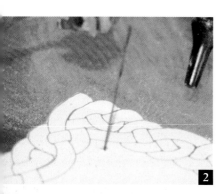

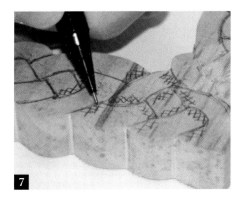

7

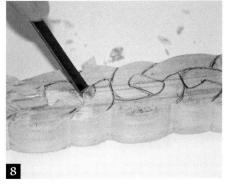

8

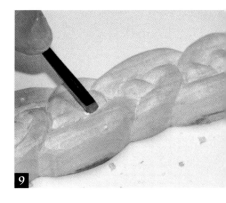

9

7 If you think you may have difficulty in identifying the thread of the weave during carving, try shading the areas that have to be reduced with a pen or pencil.

8 Lower the bands where they weave behind, and make a deep 'V' between bands that pass alongside each other.

9 Use an inverted curved gouge or a knife to round the long edges of each band, to form a rope-like shape. This will help separate the bands and define the knotwork.

10 Where a band turns sharply back on itself, use the point of a knife to cut the tiny triangle at the bend.

11 When the entire knotwork frame has been carved, reduce the area at the top, between the two bands, to a depth of 4mm ($\frac{5}{32}$in).

12 Using a scrap of 4mm ($\frac{5}{32}$in) plywood or MDF, cut out your chosen lettering template. Drill small pilot holes where necessary to make the internal cuts.

If you prefer to have the letters cut out, as described in step 4, do that at this stage. Bear in mind that the throat of your scrollsaw needs to be large enough to accommodate the length of the board.

13 Protect the frame with a clear varnish. This is particularly important if it is to be sited in a kitchen.

14 After priming the MDF backboard and lettering, apply at least two coats of blackboard paint to both.

15 To assemble the message board, glue the backboard and lettering in place.

16 As an optional extra, you can make a chalk holder for the board. To do this, take a piece of matching scrap timber measuring 40mm high x 50mm wide x 18mm deep (1$\frac{1}{2}$ x 2 x $\frac{3}{4}$in). Cut it to an 'L' shape, leaving the back 4mm ($\frac{5}{32}$in) deep and the bottom leg approx. 8mm ($\frac{5}{16}$in) deep. Make a concave groove along the top of the leg as shown on the right.

17 Cut a 4mm ($\frac{5}{32}$in) rebate into the back of the frame, at the bottom where shown, for the chalk holder to sit in, and then glue it in place. Varnish the chalk holder to match the frame.

18 To ensure that the message board doesn't move about when in use, fasten it to the wall using adhesive foam pads.

11

12

16

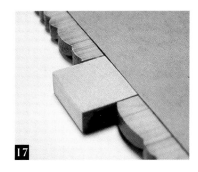

17

'Tree of Life' seed keeper

Materials

Photocopy of template 8A or 8B (page 99 or 100), and 8C (page 101), enlarged by 125%

Suitable timber measuring 270 x 160 x 12mm for backboard (10⅝ x 6¼ x ½in) (lime)

Matching timber 270 x 60 x 12mm for shelf (10⅝ x 2⅜ x ½in)

Carbon paper

Repositionable spray adhesive

2 brass screws

Wood glue

5 empty 35mm film canisters, preferably black, for seed storage

Wax or varnish finish of choice

2 picture hangers

 rees held particular significance for the Celts, with their branches reaching heavenward and their roots firmly planted in Mother Earth. Trees represented not only a link between the upper and lower world, but were also a reminder of the eternal cycle of the seasons.

The 'tree-of-life' motif is found in both pagan and Christian art, and stands as a symbol of balance and unification of the two realms. In order to incorporate the 'tree of life' into manuscript decoration, the design was often made to emerge from a pot, which symbolized Mother Earth. The tree itself was mostly portrayed as the vine and grapes, a symbol associated with Christ, which represents the resurrection and his eternal life.

The motif appears in *The Book of Kells* several times, the 'Arrest of Christ', folio 114 recto, being a good example (see Introduction, page 1). The vine and grapes appears on either side of the head of Christ as well as on the columns at either side of the picture.

Grapes frequently appear in threes, which is an important number in Celtic mythology, as it represents the trinity. Thus in this one, apparently simple motif, many layers of symbolism exist.

The 'tree-of-life' motif has been used as the basis of this project, which is designed to store seeds gathered at harvest time and preserved in the dark and dry, ready for spring planting. There are two designs to choose from, one of which is headed 'Seeds', the other 'Dochas', which translates from the Irish into 'Hope'.

2

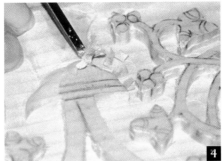

4

I chose the word because I feel that when we plant new seeds, we plant hope for the future, continuing the circle of life. Both designs are made in the same way apart from changing the letters.

For the project shown here, I used lime wood (basswood). The film canisters used are black so that the seeds can remain in the dark over winter. If preferred, they can be painted on the outside , but in that case leave the area where the lid snaps on unpainted, to ensure a good fit.

The project can easily be adapted for other storage uses, such as paper clips, push pins, sewing pins, golf tees, or even 35mm films. For some of these it would be useful to use clear plastic film canisters and in any case you would, of course, need to choose a more appropriate word than 'seeds' to identify the contents.

Method

1 Place carbon paper between your chosen template and the largest piece of timber and trace the design onto it. Cut round the outside lines.

2 Carefully reduce all the background from around the 'tree-of-life' design to a depth of 5–6mm (³/₁₆–¹/₄in). I used a router fitted with a 7mm (⁹/₃₂in) straight cutter for most of the waste removal, then used a 2mm (³/₃₂in) cutter to get to the smaller areas. If you don't have a router, the waste can be removed using chisels and gouges.

3 Next, trim along the pattern lines to produce clean vertical sides to all the branches, leaves and grapes. This will ensure that you have a good even design to work with when you round the branches. I used a chip knife to score along the lines, and then cleared the waste away using small chisels and gouges. Trim along the inside of the raised border in the same way.

4 Shape the pot from which the tree grows by rounding the sides and bowl.

5 Begin shaping the branches, starting at the point where they emerge from the pot, and working towards the ends. This way you can gradually reduce the branch depth as you go along.

6 At the point where branches weave under and over, score along the lines that cross, then use the chisel at right angles to grade down the material to give the appearance of weaving under. Only round the sides after you are satisfied with the depth of the weave.

7 As you come to a leaf, reduce the depth of it by about half, and shape the stem into it, forming an inverted 'V' where it meets the leaf.

Tools

Scrollsaw or fretsaw

Router (optional)

Chisels and gouges

Drill with bit to match brass screws

Countersink bit

32mm (1¼in) flat wood bit for hole cutting

Craft knife or chip knife

6

7

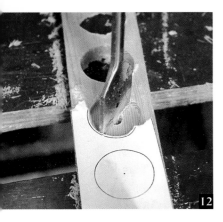 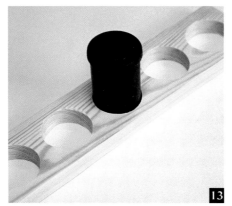 

8 As you come to a bunch of grapes, reduce the depth by only 1–2mm ($\frac{1}{16}$–$\frac{3}{32}$in) and re-draw the three circles. Cut out the small triangle formed at the centre of the circles using a chip knife or craft knife then round each of them over to form a ball shape. Again, shape the stem into the grapes. The grapes can be made to look more realistic by undercutting them slightly, using a small gouge to remove a little of the material all round the base of each cluster of grapes.

9 Mark the curved lines on each leaf, using a small gouge held vertically.

10 Tidy up the lettering, making sure that the sides are vertical. I have kept the letters at their full depth, but you can reduce them if you prefer.

11 Next, make the shelf to hold the canisters. Stick template 8C onto the smaller piece of timber, using spray adhesive, and cut to size.

12 Using the flat bit, cut out the five holes as shown. The largest flat bit available is 32mm (1$\frac{1}{4}$in), which is just slightly too small for the 34mm (1$\frac{3}{8}$in) diameter canisters, so sand them back

to size after cutting. This is easily done with a small sanding drum.

13 The shelf, ready for joining to the backboard, is shown above. Check the holes for size.

14 With the shelf held at right angles to the bottom of the backboard, where indicated on the template, drill two pilot holes for the screws. Use a countersink bit on the back of the backboard so that the screws can sit flush with the back. Hold the shelf in place in a workbench or vice, apply a layer of wood glue along the edge, then screw the backboard to it.

15 Finish the piece using either wax or varnish. If the seed keeper is going to be hung in an outbuilding, a waterproof varnish would be the most suitable finish. Attach two picture hangers to the back of the seed keeper, to ensure that it hangs firmly as the canisters are taken in and out.

16 Make a set of labels for the canisters to identify the contents of each, and stick them onto the canisters near the bottom, where they can be more easily read.

ḣanᴅ ꭑiꭉꭉoꭉ

his hand mirror introduces a new element of Celtic art, that of the spiral. The spiral, or triskele, is made up of three legs or curves that radiate from a common centre, and is thought to represent the sun and the movement of heavenly bodies. Others interpret the three coils as representing the three elements of heaven, earth and water, and a safeguard against evil.

The spiral motif appears in very early pagan Celtic art; one of the oldest examples is on the entrance stone at Newgrange in County Meath, Ireland, which dates back to 3000BC. Newgrange – a passage-tomb and the alleged burial place of the ancient Kings of Tara – is one of the most famous prehistoric monuments.

Spirals with two coils appear on early Celtic jewellery, such as bronze-age metal cloak fasteners and third-century Irish horse ornaments. These motifs are also found on stone crosses carved by stonemasons working in the sixth century.

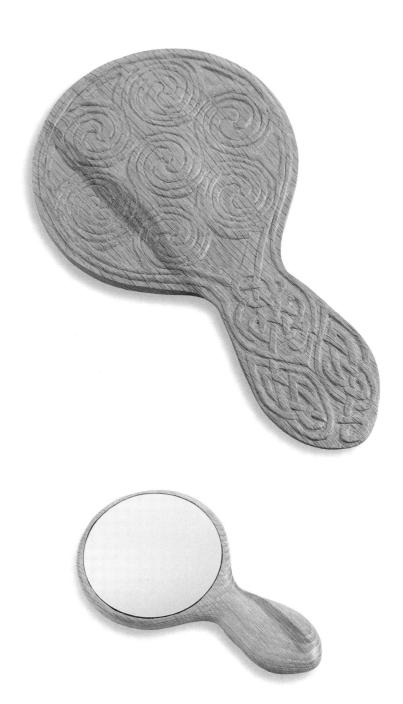

The double-sided cross slab-stone in Aberlemno churchyard, Angus

Stone at Aberlemno

Materials

Photocopy of template 9A, on page 102, enlarged by 125%

Carbon paper

Repositionable spray adhesive

Timber, at least 160 x 260 x 12mm (6¼ x 10¼ x ½in) (European oak)

Round mirror, 125mm (5in) in diameter

Glue suitable for sticking glass to timber.

Tools

Scrollsaw or hand fretsaw

Router with straight cutter (optional) and non-slip mat

Dremel with cutter bit No 9936 (optional)

Carving chisels and gouges

Chip-carving knife (optional)

Clear wax polish, or finish of your choice

Spirals appear in pictorial form in *The Book of Kells*, where the Celtic artist took the simple spiral and introduced fantastic variations by adding animal and bird features.

The mirror featured in this project follows the tradition of the enamelled and engraved bronze mirrors produced by craftsmen of the pre-Roman Celtic period of British culture.

The Celts were particularly conscious of their appearance, especially their clothes and hair, so mirrors and combs were very important objects. Many Pictish stone carvings bear a mirror and comb motif. In this drawing of another of the Aberlemno stones, the mirror and comb can be seen in the lower right-hand corner.

The actual design on the back of the mirror has been adapted from the central motif on the eighth-century High Cross of Aberlemno, Scotland, shown below.

Two legs from the lower spirals break away to create the knotwork on the handle, forming an eternal knot.

For this project, I used European oak for strength, as the handle has to be strong enough to support the weight of the mirror. Oak is not the easiest of woods to carve, as the grain is quite coarse, but the finished result makes it worth the effort.

Detail on the eighth-century High Cross of Aberlemno

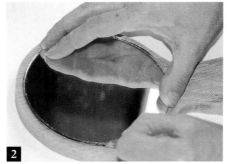

Method

1 Either trace the design for the back of the mirror frame (template 9A) through carbon paper onto the timber, and cut around the outside of it, or stick the template onto the timber for cutting out using spray adhesive, as shown here. I prefer the latter method, as I find it easier to follow a black line on white background, but it means that the design must then be traced onto the timber after cutting out.

2 Turn the mirror frame over, and position the mirror centrally on the large circle, holding it firmly in place with one hand. Draw round the mirror to mark where the rebate needs to be cut.

3 The rebate is cut to the depth of the mirror, plus an extra millimetre to allow for gluing and final sanding. A router is the obvious choice for this operation, but if you do not have access to a router or a Dremel with routing facility, the rebate can be made using chisels and gouges, making sure that the base of the rebate is smooth and even.

   Most standard routers will have to be used freehand to cut the circle, as the diameter is too small to be cut using the central pivot method. This is not a problem if both hands are used to guide the base of the router instead of using the handles. As with any routing operation, ensure that the base is kept level at all times, so that the cutting bit cuts at an even depth throughout. Use a non-slip router mat under the work to hold it in place during the routing operation.

4 Round off the outside edges, also using the router fitted with a round-over bit. Again, if no router is available, you can use a gouge, chisel, or a rotary carving tool.

5 Working still on the mirror side, shape the handle by rounding it and slimming down the 'waist' where it meets the larger circle. This can be quickly achieved using a structured tooth tungsten carbide bit in a rotary tool, but only if you are well practised in its use, and are sure of your ability to control the cutter. Otherwise, use a gouge or chip carving knife.

6 Next begin the carving on the reverse. Before starting to carve the spirals, the central line must be scored. There are several ways of doing this – the choice is yours: you can cut the shape using a gouge of the same sweep of curve, held at right angles; mark the line with a V-tool, or score it with a chip knife or craft knife.

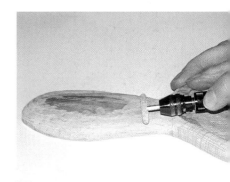

The rebate cut to fit the mirror, and the edges rounded

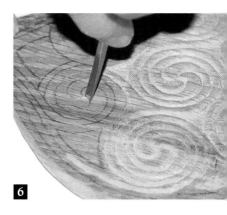

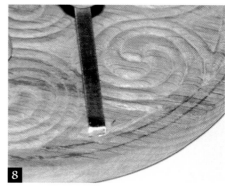

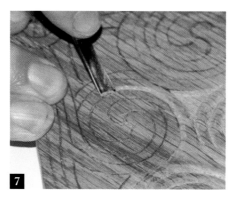

7 Deepen a V-shaped groove between the coils by removing material evenly on either side of the scored line and curve over the top of each coil as it is formed. Work at right angles to the central line, unless using a V-tool.

8 When all the spirals are complete, remove the areas between them (shown shaded on the template) to an even depth. Try to make this depth the same as the depth between the coils of the spirals.

9 Reduce the outer ring to the same depth and round over the large coil that is left enclosing the spirals.

10 Work the knotwork design on the handle in the same manner as in previous chapters, by scoring the lines then reducing the background.

11 Using a fine 5mm (³⁄₁₆in) straight chisel, reduce the raised bands on either side of each crossing point to give the effect of them weaving under and over each other.

12 When all the carving is complete, sand as appropriate and apply the finish of your choice. I used a clear wax polish, as the colour and grain of the wood needed no further enhancement. Do not apply any finish to the area where the mirror is to be glued, however, as it may prevent a good bond.

13 Glue the mirror firmly in place on the reverse side.

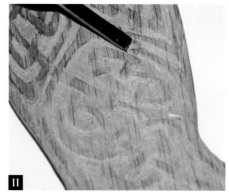

DRAGON TRINKET BOX

his project introduces a zoomorphic design in a different material: a brass dragon inset into the lid of the box. For once, there is no actual carving to be done, since the pattern is worked on the scrollsaw (or fretsaw) and with an engraving tool.

The dragon is a mythical beast that appears in many shapes and guises in Celtic folklore. Dragon pairs, 'S' shaped and placed back to back, appear in Celtic art from as early as the fourth century BC, mainly on metalwork objects such as scabbards and spears. This signifies the protective role they played.

The symbol of the dragon has particular significance in the Celtic culture of the Welsh. Since 1901 the red dragon has been adopted as a national symbol, and became part of the Welsh flag in the mid-twentieth century.

A recurrent theme throughout the history of the dragon has been one of guardianship. The dragons of fairy tales famously guard caves full of treasure, so what better symbol to protect the cherished possessions within your box.

Method

1 Use double-sided sticky tape to attach the dragon template 10A to the face of the brass. If the brass is thin, it can be stuck to a piece of scrap plywood to make cutting and handling easier. If not, stick a layer or two of masking tape to the underside of the brass to prevent damage to the saw table and to make handling easier.

Materials

Photocopies of templates 10A and 10B, on page 103

Piece of brass measuring 90 x 150mm (3½ x 6in)

Timber, 100 x 150 x 40mm (4 x 6 x 1½in)

Timber, 100 x 150 x 6mm (4 x 6 x ¼in)

2 pieces of timber, 100 x 150 x 4mm (4 x 6 x ⁵⁄₃₂in)

Double-sided sticky tape

Wood glue

General-purpose glue such as Bostick

Fast-dry enamel, matt black paint (optional)

Clear varnish

Brass polish and lacquer

Repositionable spray adhesive

Tools

Scrollsaw or fretsaw

Drill fitted with 2mm (³⁄₃₂in) bit

Rotary tool fitted with small engraving bit

2 Drill pilot holes in the shaded areas of the dragon design to allow the internal cuts to be made.

3 Using a fine-toothed blade and half speed, cut out all the internal waste.

4 When all the internal waste has been removed, cut around the outside of the dragon motif.

5 Whilst the template is still attached to the brass motif, use the small engraving bit fitted in a rotary tool to carefully engrave the lines that make up the rest of the design. The engraving bit will cut through the paper onto the brass, but the presence of the paper will stop the bit from slipping.

6 Remove the template and sticky tape and file any sharp edges as necessary.

7 Polish the brass and, if desired, define the engraved lines by going over them with a fine, black, waterproof ink

drawing pen. When this is dry, it is a necessary to apply a coat of lacquer to prevent oxidization.

8 Use double-sided tape to stack the 6mm (¼in) piece of timber onto the 40mm (1½in) piece of timber, and then stick the box template, 10B, onto the top using spray adhesive. Cut around the outside of the box.

9 Separate the top from the bottom, peel off the template, and re-apply it to the top of the 40mm (1½in) deep piece of timber, which will form the body of the box.

10 Drill a pilot hole inside the inner line; thread the saw blade through, then cut around the inner line, to form the straight sides of the box.

11 Place the body of the box onto each of the 4mm (⁵⁄₃₂in) pieces of timber in turn and draw round the inside of the box to make a base and a rebate for the lid.

12 Glue one of the pieces into the base of the box and leave to dry.

13 To make the lid, place the brass dragon motif centrally on the top of the lid and draw round the outside, but don't go into every indentation, make the line a smooth, general outline.

14 Reduce the depth of the wood inside this line to match the depth of the brass motif. This can be done with a chisel or gouge, or a router if you have one. Make sure that the surface is left smooth and even.

15 Paint the inside of this rebate matt black to create a strong contrast to the brass. If you have chosen a dark timber this may not be necessary.

16 When dry, glue the brass in place in the rebate.

17 Glue the remaining 4mm (⁵⁄₃₂in) timber shape to the underside of the lid to form an artificial rebate that will hold it in place when it sits on top of the box.

18 To complete the box, apply two coats of clear varnish, inside and out.

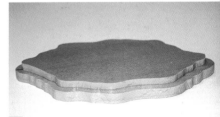

KNOTWORK JIGSAW BOXES

his challenging piece comprises a set of five lidded boxes, which link together in a jigsaw fashion. The greatest challenge is to fit all the boxes back together in their correct place, with their matching lids, when the project is finished.

Once all the boxes are set up together, the knotwork decoration on the lids forms one continuous thread weaving from box to box, so reinforcing the link. The continuity is intentional, a symbol of eternity.

The equal-armed cross with interlace is a common element of Celtic decoration, and occurs on several pages of *The Book of Kells*, most prominently flanking the figure of Christ and St John (see page viii, facing the Introduction).

Several elaborate book covers and book shrines also feature this design in embossed metalwork and the notable cross slab-stone of Ulbster in Caithness, Scotland, also bears the same pattern.

For this project I have used a man-made material, medium density fibreboard (MDF). I chose this partly because it is readily available in the thickness needed, partly because it is extremely easy to work, and also because I wanted to use a paint finish. As always when using man-made materials, particularly MDF, dust masks must be worn at all times, due to the resins that are used in the manufacturing process. (You will find advice on workshop safety generally, including precautions to take when using MDF, on pages 8–9.)

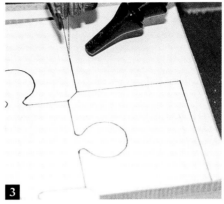

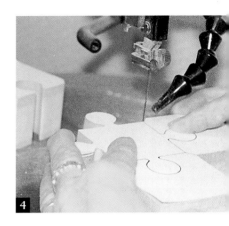

Method

1 First prepare for cutting, by stacking the three pieces of MDF and firmly fixing them together using double-sided sticky tape between the layers. Place the 4mm (⁵⁄₃₂in) piece at the bottom, the 30mm (1⅛in) in the middle, then the 6mm (¼in) on top. These will be the box components of base, body and lid respectively.

2 Stick the box template 11A onto the top using spray adhesive. The boxes are now ready to be cut out on the scrollsaw but, before beginning, use a set square to check that the blade is perfectly vertical as, if it is even slightly out of true, you will only be able to slide the boxes up or down in one direction instead of both.

3 Cut round the outside of all the boxes first, before attempting to separate the jigsaw shapes.

4 Very carefully cut out the jigsaw shapes. Each has to be done in one sweep to give a good clean single cut, so take care negotiating the corners and curves. If you are not completely confident about it, practise by making some spare template copies and cutting them out using waste pieces of MDF. You will soon become

confident enough to tackle the real thing. Fortunately MDF is inexpensive, so it's not the end of the world if you do make a mistake.

5 When all four 'arms' have been separated from the centre box, mark each part of each box with the same letter or number. This makes it easier to identify the correct pieces when it comes to reconstructing it all. Carefully separate the three layers of MDF on all five boxes.

6 Taking the middle section of each box, mark a line 4mm (⁵⁄₃₂in) in from the edge. The centre will be cut out to make the box cavity. The four 'arm' boxes can be cut following the whole box shape, but for the central box just cut a square and do not attempt to cut into the protruding circles (unless you're a complete masochist). Template 11B, on page 105, shows how it should look.

Drill a pilot hole in the middle waste area, thread the scrollsaw blade through and cut along the marked line.

7 Make a rebate to hold the lids in place from the spare 4mm (⁵⁄₃₂in) MDF. Using the box body as a template, draw a line round the inside of the

Tools
Dust mask

Scrollsaw or hand fretsaw

Small chisels and gouges

Drill

Craft knife or chip knife

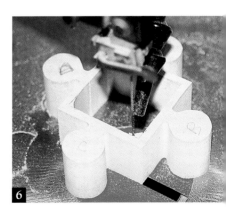

7

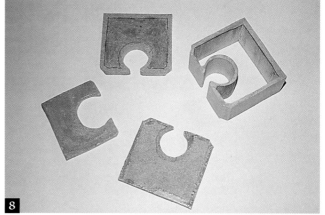

8

cavity onto the MDF, numbering each piece to its corresponding box. Cut these out using the scrollsaw or hand fretsaw.

8 Assemble each box, using impact adhesive to give a strong bond. Apply a layer of glue, 4mm (⁵⁄₃₂in) wide, to the edges of the base to correspond to the walls of the box, and to the underside of the middle section. Press together when dry, according to the manufacturer's instructions. Glue

the rebate to the underside of the lid, making sure that the lid will sit correctly on the box before applying final pressure to the join. Above you can see the four sections of the box glued and ready to assemble.

9 Assemble the five boxes into their finished shape, so that the knotwork design can be transferred to the lids. The best way to do this is to stick a photocopy of template 11C to some carbon paper using spray adhesive, then cut round the outside of the design. Use masking tape to hold this in place on the boxes and trace the design onto the lids. Lift the template in a few places to make sure the design has transferred successfully before removing it completely.

10 All the carving is done whilst the boxes are joined, so that the lines of the knotwork follow smoothly from one lid to the next. Take a sharp chip knife or craft knife and first score along the pencil lines. Next, very carefully reduce the background between the ribbons, using a small gouge. Ideally, the background should be reduced to a depth of 2–3mm (³⁄₃₂–¹⁄₈in).

9

12

11 Once all the background has been reduced, create the weaving effect of the interlacing by reducing the ribbons on either side of each crossover point. Always be mindful of the way the ribbons weave regularly under and over.

12 In the photograph above you can see the progression of the carving, clockwise from the top: the design has been scored along the lines, the next lid has had the background reduced, next shows the 'weaving' completed, and the final lid has been sanded and is ready to be painted.

13 Paint all the parts of the box with primer. Always use a primer that is compatible with the final finish. When the primer is dry sand it smooth, as it will have raised the fibres of the MDF. Apply two coats of cream emulsion paint, or whatever base colour you choose. When this is dry, apply the blue paint (or whatever colour you prefer) to the background.

14 If your skills with a fine paintbrush are limited, you may find the following method useful: take a wax candle and rub it over the raised surfaces of the knotwork, making sure all areas are fully covered.

15 Next, paint in between the knotwork without worrying if you get paint on the top surfaces. When the paint is dry remove the wax by rubbing down with a very fine grade of steel wool, preferably 0000. This should leave the two colours separate, with a slightly distressed type of finish.

16 Apply a thin application of clear wax polish to all the outside surfaces, so that the boxes slide apart easily.

All that remains is for you to put the boxes back together. Good luck!

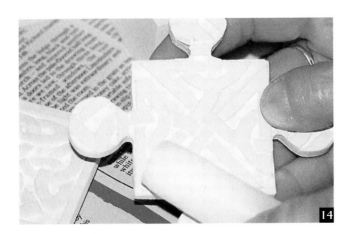

14

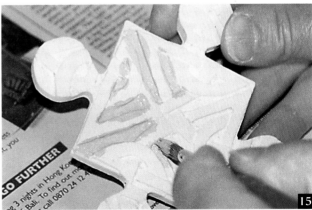

15

Celtic cross

The design of carved stone crosses evolved over thousands of years, an amalgam of many concepts and cultures. There are influences from the standing stones of solar cults, from the cross carvings on 'ancestor stones' dating back to 10,000BC France, through to the Christianization of the West in the sixth century. Although the cross shape is most obviously associated with Christianity, the Callanish Stones in Scotland are arranged in the form of a Celtic Cross, (a cross with a ring surrounding it), and pre-date Christianity by at least 2,000 years.

The ringed cross is a particularly strong and striking image in Celtic art. It is thought that the design came about when early missionaries carved crosses onto standing stones, which had been pagan objects of worship, rather than alienating their potential converts by pulling them down. From there, slab-stones were purposely carved to take cross designs, and then the slab-stones themselves were carved into cross shapes.

The roadside cross-slab at Aberlemno, Scotland (see top right), is a fine example of an eighth-century ring cross carved onto a stone slab.

Elaborate knotwork and spiral designs began appearing on the cross faces, then later Irish crosses depicted scenes from the scriptures, which would have been useful teaching aids in a world where the written word was not familiar to the masses. Pictish slab-stone crosses often depicted battle scenes on the back. The great cross-slab in Aberlemno graveyard in Scotland is said to be a depiction of the Battle of Nechtansmere that had been fought nearby in AD685 (see below left).

Several stone crosses have bosses carved on them, which have no function other than to represent nail heads that would have been on wooden crosses. I have incorporated a small boss at the centre of my design.

The freestanding, ringed cross design developed in Ireland, but is found in other Celtic societies, and many fine examples can be seen in Scotland. St Columba travelled from Glencolumbkille on the northwest coast of Ireland in the sixth century and established a monastery on the small island of Iona off the coast of Scotland. Many elaborate stone crosses were carved at this time, but tragically, puritanical zealots of the sixteenth century destroyed a huge number, with over 150 being thrown into the seas off Iona and other islands alone.

The 'ring' element of the ringed cross is widely recognized as a solar symbol. Many interpretations have been ascribed to the design as a whole, one of which suggests that the four points at which the cross and ring intersect represent the four seasons, which the Celts knew as Imbolc (spring), Beltaine (summer), Lugnasadh (autumn) and Samhain (winter). This fits in neatly with the solar symbolism of the circle motif.

The stepped base is similar to the one supporting St Martin's Cross on Iona (shown far right), and I have made it deliberately rugged to contrast with the detailed symmetry of the cross itself.

Cross-slab at Aberlemno, Scotland

St Martin's Cross, Iona

Cross-slab in Aberlemno graveyard

2

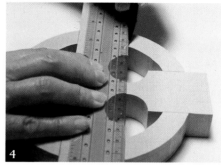

4

Materials

Photocopy of template 12A on page 107, enlarged by 125%

Timber for cross: 280 x 180 x at least 25mm (11 x 7 x 1in) (lime)

Timber for base: 110 x 90 x 45mm (4½ x 3½ x 1¾in) (lime)

Repositionable spray adhesive

Carbon paper

Wax polish, or preferred finish

Wood glue

Tools

Plane (optional – if required)

Medium or fine sandpaper (120 or 180 grades)

Scrollsaw, fretsaw or electric jigsaw

Drill with wood bit

Metal rule

Sharp knife

Chisels and gouges

In this project the cross is carved on both the back and front faces, so that it can be viewed from both sides, but you may prefer to carve just one face.

Method

1 Ensure that both sides of the timber for the cross are perfectly smooth and even – if not, plane where necessary and sand with medium or fine sandpaper. Stick the template onto one side of the timber using spray adhesive.

2 Drill pilot holes into each of the central shaded areas of the design to allow blade access, and make the internal cuts.

Make sure that the points where the ring and cross meet are sharp, by cutting in from opposite directions – do not cut the corner in one sweep, as this would round it.

3 When all the internal cuts have been made, cut out around the outside and then remove the template.

4 Draw in the lines where the cross intersects the ring, on both back and front of the cross, using a ruler for accuracy.

5 On the outside edge of the ring, draw two lines around the circumference, each 5mm (³⁄₁₆in) in from the front and back as shown. These lines indicate the depth to which the ring must be reduced, so that the cross stands proud.

6 To reduce the depth of the ring by this amount, score along the lines on the face of the cross, then use a chisel or gouge to remove the waste from the front and back, as shown.

7 Trace the design onto the arms of the cross and ring on both sides, using carbon paper between the template and wood. You will find it easier to cut out the ring sections of the template before transferring them.

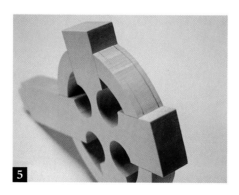

5

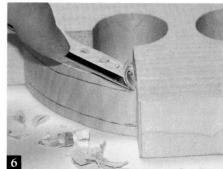

6

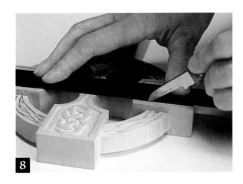

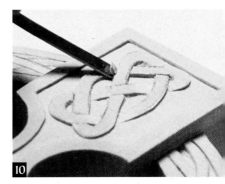

The mortice and tenon joint used to join the cross to the base

8 Use a metal rule and sharp knife to score along the straight lines.

9 Score along the lines of the knotwork design, then reduce all the background material to the same depth. This can be 1–2mm ($\frac{1}{16}$–$\frac{3}{32}$in) as preferred.

10 Create the weaving effect by reducing the material on either side of the crossing points, as in projects 3, 5 and 11.

11 Next, round over the sides of the central boss.

12 Complete the tenon at the base of the cross, by taking 5mm ($\frac{3}{16}$in) off the back and front of the bottom extension.

13 Use the remaining piece of timber to make the base. Cut in two steps on all four sides and then round off the shoulders of the steps.

14 On the top of the base, cut in a mortice joint the same size and depth as the tenon.

15 Glue the cross onto the base and, when dry, finish with two or three coats of wax polish, or as preferred.

Fun photo frame

Materials

Photocopies of templates 13A, 13B and 13C on page 108

Suitable timber measuring 160 x 110 x 25mm (6¼ x 4¼ x 1in) (sycamore)

N.B. See note about direction of grain in stage 1.

Repositionable spray adhesive

Carbon paper

Approx 100mm (4in) of narrow cord or string

Acetate if required

Impact adhesive

Clear wax and baby toothbrush, or preferred finish

Tacks

aving tackled some of the previous projects, you can now relax and have some fun with this small, chunky, photo frame. I have based the design on a dog, which appears in various forms in Celtic art.

Dogs had great symbolic significance in Celtic folklore: they were associated with healing and protection and would invariably accompany their masters into battle, or on fantastic journeys. Such was their importance that they appeared in almost every type of Celtic art and legend, including epic tales, illuminated manuscripts, metalwork and stone carvings.

The eighth century St Andrew's sarcophagus in Fife, Scotland, showing several hunting dogs carved in high relief

In the design used for this project, the arms of the dog are fairly normal, not intertwined as might be expected, but the legs are something else altogether. The interlacing of the legs is taken over by cords to which the feet are attached; these in turn dangle over the top of the photo, and it is almost as if the toes are pointing to the picture contained in the frame.

The chunkiness of the frame enables it to be freestanding and self-supporting.

I used sycamore for the project, but it works well if you use two contrasting timbers for the dog and frame, as you can see on the facing page, where dark curly jarra was used for the dog, and sycamore for the frame.

Method

1 Stick the three templates onto the timber using spray adhesive, ensuring that the grain runs vertically. The feet need to be considerably thinner than the frame and dog, just 3–4mm (1/8–5/32in) thick, so you could cut one foot at 25mm (1in) thick from your block of wood, then slice off two sections the required depth with a fretsaw.

2 Using a scrollsaw or hand fretsaw, cut out the dog, frame and foot.

3 Drill small pilot holes for the blade to make the internal cuts for the dog (template 13B). The areas of the dog to remove are the three shaded areas on the template between the tail, the two sections separating the legs and the gap in the belly.

4 Drill pilot holes for the internal cuts in the frame (template 13A).

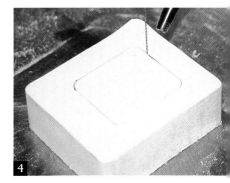

The components cut out ready to begin the shaping

6

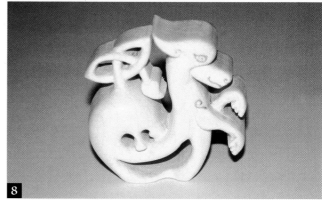

8

5 Slip some carbon paper between the template and the wood and transfer the remaining design lines onto the surface of the dog.

6 Begin shaping the dog: reduce the depth of the tail by removing about 10mm (⅜in), leaving a depth of about 15mm (⅝in). For this I used a structured-tooth tungsten carbide cutter in a rotary tool, but small chisels or gouges could also be used effectively. Keep the tail area flat for now, as this makes it easier to create the weaving effect later, but curve the area of the body where it meets the tail to give a nice rounded back. Continue curving all the edges of the body except the base, which needs to be kept flat for attaching to the frame.

7 Reduce the depth of the top arm, so that it appears to be behind the lower arm, and curve the edges over to give a rounded look. This can be done with either small gouges, a knife – such as a chip carving knife – or even a craft knife. Remove a little of the body below the lower arm to create something of an armpit for definition, and again curve the arm into a smooth rounded shape. Reduce the depth of the arm towards the 'wrist' so that the paw can be given definition.

8 Remove about 5mm (³⁄₁₆in) from the leg that is nearest the centre, at the point where it meets the back of the dog. Gradually slope it back up towards the rump, curving the sides at the same time, to make it look as if it is weaving behind the back of the dog. Then remove a similar amount of material from below the other leg to make it appear to weave in front of the body. Keeping the base of the leg flat, curve the sides of the leg and body in between the legs.

9 Score along the line that separates the snout from the head, and then reduce the snout by about 3mm (⅛in) and curve over the edges.

10 Curve the edges of the rest of the head, including the step that was created when reducing the snout. Remove some of the material below the ear at the back of the neck, to give it greater definition. Curve the top edge of the ear and taper the tip down slightly.

11 Ensure that all the remaining edges of the body have been curved over to give a really smooth finish, including the section of the belly that has been cut out.

12 Now carve the knotwork on the tail. Transfer the guidelines onto the tail to mark the weaving. Score along the lines using either a knife, or a gouge that has the same curve as the line, and then reduce the material on either side of these lines, as in the previous projects.

13 Make the end of the tail into a heart shape, by reducing down the last section of tail before it goes into the heart shape, and notching a 'V' shape at this point. Curve over all the sides along the length of the tail.

14 The feet need to be shaped by curving over the sides and toes, but take care with your fingers, as they are very tiny pieces to work with – a pair of long-nosed pliers can be used to grip the feet, if preferred.

15 Before adding the final features, give the dog a good sanding to make it really smooth and curvy. Draw in the eye, mouth, nose and shoulder curl lines first, and then indent along the lines. I used a small V-tool for this, but a chip or craft knife could also be used.

16 The final job is to make a shape in the base for the cord of the leg to weave forward. Do this by cutting out a small semi-circular shape at the bottom of the body, directly below the centre of the leg.

17 The cord for the legs is just pressed into the holes, rather than threaded through the wood. Drill the holes with a bit corresponding to the diameter of the cord, in this case 1mm (¹⁄₁₆in), and make them only about 1.5mm (approx. ¹⁄₁₆in) deep, just enough to glue the cord into. Drill a hole in the top edge of each foot,

and through the underside of the belly cutout at a point below the centre leg, about 5mm (³⁄₁₆in) in from the edge. The photo below shows the position of the holes, both on the protruding leg and through the base immediately below this.

18 Cut two pieces of cord approximately 40mm (1½in) long and glue a foot to one end of each. Assess the final length of the cord by holding it against the dog, allowing a small piece extra to fit into the drilled hole, then cut to length, 25–32mm (1–1¹³⁄₁₆in). Thread one cord through the hole in the base and glue into place in the protruding leg. Glue the other piece of cord into the hole below the centre leg, allowing it to dangle in the groove below.

19 Now work on the frame. Begin by drawing a line on the back, 5mm (³⁄₁₆in) in from the edge of the cutout. This will be the rebate to take the photograph. Rebate this edge to a depth of 12mm (½in), to bring the photograph closer to the front of the frame. If you have a router, fit a small straight cutter and, securing the frame firmly to your workbench, rout the rebate in a series of cuts, taking 3mm (¹⁄₈in) off at a time.

One way of making sure that your router stays level is to cut out the shape of the frame from the centre of a piece of 25mm (1in) MDF, slot the frame into it, then clamp this to the workbench.

If you don't have access to a router, then it is possible to use a router attachment and straight router bit for the Dremel. Failing either of these options, you can form a rebate using a chisel.

20 Cut a backing piece to hold the photo in place in the rebate – the easiest way is to draw around the rebate onto the backing piece. If desired, you can also cut a piece of acetate the same size to go in front of the photo.

21 Curve the front edges of the frame and cutout section, and sand to give a smooth finish.

22 Glue the dog in place on the top of the frame, with the legs dangling over the front. I used an impact adhesive for this, as it needs to be a really strong bond.

20

23 Give the completed frame a suitable finish: I applied a clear wax with a soft baby toothbrush, to get in all the little crevices.

24 Put your chosen photo in the rebate, with acetate in front if being used, then fasten the backing piece in place behind with a small tack top and bottom.

Mirrored Candle Sconce

t is said that there are two ways of spreading light, 'to be the candle, or the mirror that reflects it'.

This project uses mirrors to reflect the candlelight many times; the larger mirror offers a continuous reflection and, as the candle burns lower, so the lower mirrors reflect the flame. This way, one small flame can spread its light in many directions.

Candlelight does more than dispel darkness: it represents powerful symbolism in many faiths. Candles are lit for remembrance, for worship, for purity and to represent Christ as the light of the world.

Knotwork links the mirrors at the sides, and the spiral motif brings together the three elements of the sconce. The number three was very significant in Celtic art, as can be seen in the triplication of many stone-carved deities, as well as on the decorated pages of manuscripts.

Just for good measure, there is also a small amount of architectural-style carving involved in the arches, which show up to good effect when the candle is lit, throwing shadows onto the curves.

Christmas tree candles are ideal for this project, not only because of their perfect size, but also because they burn without dripping wax.

Tools

Scrollsaw or fretsaw

Chisels and gouges

Drill

Scalpel

Craft knife or chip knife
(optional)

Materials

Photocopies of templates 14A and 14B on pages 109–10

Repositionable spray adhesive

Carbon paper

Timber measuring: 230 x 170 x 10mm for back (9 x 6¹¹⁄₁₆ x ³⁄₈in) (lime)

40 x 40 x 120mm for sides (1⁹⁄₁₆ x 1⁹⁄₁₆ x 4¾in) (sycamore)

170 x 40 x 10mm for shelf (6¹¹⁄₁₆ x 1⁹⁄₁₆ x ³⁄₈in)

Spare timber for carving jig

1 mirror measuring 160 x 68mm (6¼ x 2⅝in)

8 mirror squares measuring 18 x 18mm (¾ x ¾in)

12 round mirrors 13mm (½in) in diameter

Metal tree-candleholder with spike in base

Tree-candle 100mm long x 11mm diameter (4 x ½in)

Heatproof varnish

Stone glue (or similar suitable to glue glass to wood)

Wood glue

8 brass screws

1 brass picture hanger and 2 small brass screws

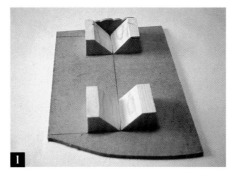

Method

1 First make a carving jig, to rest the sidepieces on whilst they are being carved. The jig can be made out of scraps of timber or MDF as follows: cut four wedges of wood approx. 45 x 30 x 50mm long (1¾ x 1¼ x 2in) and make a slope of 45° on one side along the length, to make a wedge shape. Take a piece of board approx. 280 x 200mm (11 x 8in) and mark a line down the centre about 200mm (8in) long. Glue the wedges in pairs at either end of this line, so that the slopes form 'V' shapes into which the sides can sit. Glue and nail a piece of scrap wood across the end of one V-shaped block to form an end stop.

2 Take the piece of timber measuring 230 x 170 x 10mm and stick template 14A onto it using spray adhesive.

3 Drill a pilot hole to allow for the internal cut to be made. Cut out the shaded area, keeping good sharp edges where the circle comes in to a point.

4 Cut round the rectangular outside edges of the mirror frame.

5 Turn the piece over and position the larger, rectangular, mirror over the central cut out area. Draw around the mirror's edges, then use a router or chisel to make a rebate for the mirror to sit in. Check for fit – the mirror should be flush with the outer frame when in position – then put the mirror safely to one side.

6 Position template 14A on the front of the wood, slip in some carbon paper, then trace on the design.

7 Identify the ten triangular shapes at the top of the arch and score along the lines. Reduce the depth of each triangle by 3mm (⅛in), keeping the sides vertical to ensure a uniform slope. Once you have carved the base triangle, you will have the line to join up to the top of the slope.

8 Lightly score a line from the corner of each triangle out to where it meets the corner of the next triangle. This will give a guide for where the sloping edges will come together. Chamfer down from the line of the outer triangle to the base of the inner triangle to form a uniform slope all round, following the sweep of the curves.

9 Lightly score the two lines at the base of the cutout area, and then slope across the base down to 4mm ($\frac{5}{32}$in) from the back.

10 Slope the sides in the same manner.

11 Slope the inner edge of the part-circle at the top of the cutout area.

12 Cut out the small triangle above the central spiral, sloping all three sides in towards the centre.

13 Carve the spiral by scoring along the lines using a V-tool or a knife, then make them into 'valleys'.

14 Three spiral legs will stand out from the carved valleys, which can then be rounded over to complete the spiral motif.

15 Carve the two smaller spiral motifs in a similar way, but reduce the area between the trumpets and spirals by about 1mm ($\frac{1}{16}$in). These two motifs are quite small and I found it easier to use a scalpel to shape them.

16 Prepare the sides by cutting diagonally through the square length of 40 x 40mm timber. This can be difficult without the right saw, in which case the alternative is to rest a square section of timber in the carving jig and plane down to

A completed small spiral motif is shown at the top of the picture on the left

form a triangular shape. Two lengths of timber will be needed for this. Cut each side to length, matching the length of the carved backboard as far as the line at the base of the carving.

17 Place one of the sides in the carving jig for support and, using carbon paper, transfer the design from template 14B onto the surface. Begin the carving by making four, square rebates for the mirrors. The depth of the rebates should be 1mm (¹⁄₁₆in) greater than the thickness of the mirror tile.

18 Reduce the background around the knotwork and outside of the spiral motif by 1mm (¹⁄₁₆in), leaving the narrow outside border raised also.

19 Create the weaving effect on the knotwork in the usual manner.

20 Position the small round mirrors in between the knotwork where indicated on the template and draw round them as a guide.

21 Make a round rebate equal to the depth of the mirror.

22 Carve the top spiral in the same way as for the backboard (see stages 13–14).

23 Carve the other side in the same way, making sure that it slopes in the opposite direction from the first side.

24 Glue all the small mirrors in place in their rebates.

25 Drill a hole in the shelf for the spike of the candleholder. I had to offset mine towards the front, as the diameter of the candleholder was wider than the shelf. If the spike is longer than 10mm (³⁄₈in), cut off any surplus flush with the underside of the shelf.

26 The components can now be assembled.

27 Glue the shelf in place at the bottom and use two screws through from the back to hold it firmly.

28 Glue the two sidepieces in place and use screws from behind and below to hold them firmly.

29 Varnish the timber using heatproof varnish for safety.

30 On the back of the sconce, cut a rebate behind the hanging plate to allow it to pass over a screw, and then screw the hanging plate in place, making sure that the screws used are shorter than the carved depth of the wood.

31 Finally, glue the remaining larger mirror in place and place a candle in the holder. As the candle burns down, its flame will be reflected in the lower mirrors.

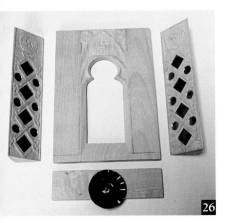

Zoomorphic Lovespoon

 or the Claddagh Lovespoon featured on page 20, I put my own interpretation of an Irish theme into what started as a very Welsh tradition. I hope I can be forgiven therefore for taking the process one step further by introducing a zoomorphic theme. There are very few project patterns available that bring new approaches to old themes, so I hope this will open up new possibilities for people wanting to create Celtic designs.

The bird in this design is taken from *The Lindisfarne Gospels*, but similar bird ornaments appear in *The Book of Kells* and on Pictish stone carvings.

The Celts perceived the different aspects of birds' abilities and behaviours as symbolic in various ways. Birds could be the bearers of messages or the portents of omens good and bad. They possessed wide-ranging traits, from beautiful singing and graceful swimming, to destruction with talon and beak.

The ability to fly was something that early man could not contemplate, so this in itself gave rise to many mythological beliefs. Only birds could bridge the space between the worlds of heaven, earth and water, and they were revered for that reason.

Materials

Photocopy of template 15A on page 111, enlarged by 125%

Timber measuring approx. 260 x 60 x 12mm (10¼ x 2⅜ x ½in) (lime)

Repositionable spray adhesive

Fine grade sandpaper (180) or fine steel wool

Carbon paper

Wax polish or preferred finish

Tools

Scrollsaw or hand fretsaw

Rotary tool fitted with no 9936 Dremel bit (optional)

Chip knife or craft knife

Chisels and gouges

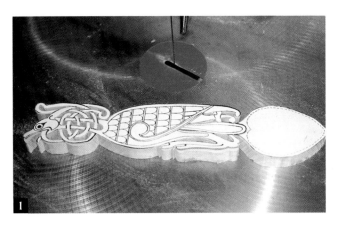

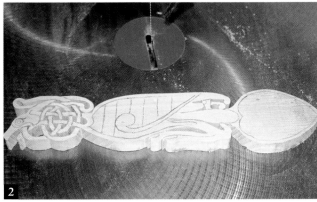

Method

1 Stick the template to the prepared smooth surface of the timber, using spray adhesive. Drill pilot holes in all the shaded areas of the template to allow the scrollsaw blade to enter, and then make the internal cuts to remove the waste.

2 Remove the template and sand off any glue residue using fine grade sandpaper, then reposition the template, slip some carbon paper underneath it, and trace the design onto the timber.

3 Shape the spoon by curving the back into a convex shape. I used a structured tooth bit in my Dremel, but would only recommend doing so if you are experienced in its use. Otherwise gouges will do the job perfectly well.

4 Shape the front of the spoon bowl into a concave shape, using the dotted line as a guide to where to start the downward slope. At this stage I prefer to just give the basic shape to the bowl and return to the final finish when the rest of the spoon is carved. The simple reason for this is that, if I make any irreversible errors, then all the time spent on the bowl is not wasted.

5 Begin to shape the bird by reducing the depth of the knotwork design at the neck. I used a structured tungsten bit in my Dremel to remove the bulk, then finished off with a gouge. Try to make a slope where the two neckpieces join the body and head, but keep the rest of the knotwork area as flat and even as possible. If you follow the bands of the pattern you will notice that the ear lappet actually becomes the tongue.

6 Using a sharp chip knife or craft knife score along the wing from the large circle to the tip. Shape the leg and tail feathers below this point by reducing the depth by 2mm (³⁄₃₂in) overall, then allowing it to rise up again towards the spoon bowl. Round the sides of the leg and toes and use a V-tool to mark the division between the front two toes, making the front toe slightly lower than the rear one. The toe at the back of the foot has to appear to weave under the main tail feather, over the middle feather then back under the rear feather. Do this by reducing the material either side of each weave, as in previous projects, but make the side of the toe rounded and keep the feathers flat in contrast.

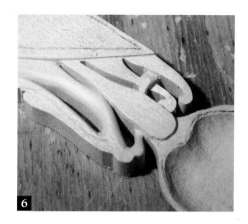

6

7 Form the claws by cutting a groove into the line of each cuticle and curving the claw and surrounding toe. These can be exaggerated to make them effective.

8 Score along the line that encloses the body feathers, then reduce the whole section inside the line by 2mm (³⁄₃₂in). Ensure that the surface of this area is smooth, then transfer the design for the feathers back onto the wood. Score along the straight lines between the layers of feathers then use a curved gouge at right angles to score the bottom of each feather.

9 Make the vertical line between the feathers using a V-tool, sharp chip knife, or craft knife.

10 Remove the small triangles of material between the bottom of the feathers.

11 Round off the front chest of the bird, allowing it to meet up with the curve of the leg.

8

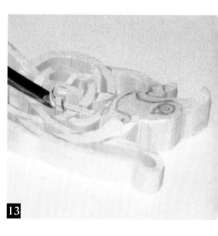

13

12 Trace on the knotwork design of the neck and score along the lines in the usual way.

13 Reduce the wood on either side of each band where it weaves under another. When all the knotwork has been completed, round off the sides of the bands.

14 Shape the head by reducing the depth of the top beak, so that the head can be curved, and reducing the lower beak behind the tongue. Round off the edges of the head to make it meet up with the curves of the neck and ear lappet. Draw in the eye and line of the jaw, and curl of the ear, then mark them out with a V-tool or sharp knife.

15 Complete the carving on the bowl of the spoon, then sand smooth.

16 Wax or oil the finished lovespoon, as preferred. I gave mine an aged appearance by applying a dark wax on top of a clear wax, than wiping it off before it dries. The dark wax stays in the grooves after polishing, accentuating the design.

17 Drill a small hole in the back in order to hang the lovespoon on a nail if required.

Coasters in holder

Materials

Photocopies of templates
16A and 16B (page 112),
and designs 16C–16H as
required, on page 113,
enlarged by 125%

Piece of timber approx.
630 x 100 x 6mm (25 x 4
x ¼in) for coaster bases
(American tulipwood)

Piece of timber approx.
110 x 110 x 50mm (4⅜ x
4⅜ x 2in) for holder
(beech)

Contrasting veneers, at
least 100 x 100mm (4 x
4in), two per design

Wood glue

Repositionable spray
adhesive

Fine garnet sandpaper

White spirit and lintfree
cloth

Waterproof ink drawing
pen (fine)

Double-sided sticky tape

Heatproof varnish

his set of six coasters is
made up of knotwork and
spiral designs, with no
carving involved. Instead
of using three-dimensional techniques as
in previous projects, I have used
contrasting veneers to give life to the
designs, which are then set into a
recessed base. I have included a wooden
holder to store the coasters.

The method I have used to make the
coasters and holder is specifically
designed to show that, if care is taken,
round objects can be made without the
use of a lathe, which would be the more
obvious choice of power tool for this
project. I have used power tools such as
a scrollsaw and router, which not
everyone will have access to, but all the
steps could be worked using hand tools.

If you do have a lathe, use the usual
turning methods to produce the bases
and holder, then make the veneered
patterns as shown.

Using two contrasting veneers for each
design will produce two versions of the
same design reversed. This means that a
set of six coasters can be made using just
three of the designs, or two sets of
coasters could be made with six differing
designs in each set, and each set
contrasting with the other. The patterns
chosen for the coasters have been kept
simple, to reduce the number of cuts
needed, to cater for those who have not
used veneers before. When the technique
has been practised and mastered on these
simplified designs, you could go on to
make your own designs using more
complicated patterns.

  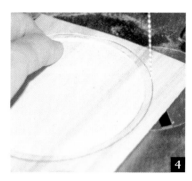

Method

1 Sand both sides of the timber that will be used for the coaster bases and use a pair of compasses to draw out six coasters, using template 16A as a guide to help you set the radius of the inner and outer circles.

2 Set the router at a depth to match the depth of the veneer, plus a little extra to allow for gluing and sanding. In my case it was 0.7mm in total. If it is not possible to use a circle guide with your router because of the small circumference, hold the base plate of the router instead of the handles to gain more control. Rout out the central section of each holder up to the inner line. It is easier to rout the bases before they are cut out individually, as shown, as this gives the router base a bigger area for support.

3 If necessary, tidy up the routed edges with a sharp knife. It is a good idea to rout just inside the final line if you are in any doubt about being able to cut accurately to the line, and you can then cut back to the line with a knife.

4 Cut out the six discs, following the outer line, using a scrollsaw, jigsaw or fretsaw.

5 Choose one of the motifs and make two photocopies. Stick a template to each of two contrasting coloured veneers, using a spray adhesive.

6 Using a sharp craft knife and cutting board, carefully cut round the design, **but do NOT cut any of the crossing lines of the knotwork patterns**.

As each section is cut, cut the same section of the contrasting veneer and gradually rebuild the pattern by

Tools

Scrollsaw or hand fretsaw

Router with straight bit or chisel

Sharp craft knife, scalpel or chip carving knife

Compasses

swapping the cut pieces. The cuts must be made to follow the lines of the design accurately, so that the pieces will fit back together perfectly when swapped.

7 Spread a thin, even layer of glue into the routed area of the coaster base and carefully stick the re-assembled pattern into place. Some varieties of wood veneers can cockle quite easily, for example the burr veneer used in the spiral motif, so apply pressure for as long as necessary to make sure all the parts of the veneer stick firmly.

8 The fine corners are susceptible to breakage when the grain runs across the design, which is unavoidable, so make any necessary repairs to the veneers using small offcuts.

Don't be put off if the coaster looks a little disappointing at this stage. Leave it to dry thoroughly then gently sand it level using fine garnet paper. Clean with a little white spirit on a lint-free cloth and the fresh colours of the veneers will be revealed.

9 Draw in the remaining lines of the design using a fine, waterproof ink drawing pen, then give each coaster two coats of heat-resistant varnish, rubbing down gently between coats. Varnish the bottom and sides as well, to prevent any movement of the wood.

10 Cut out two or five more designs in the same way, depending on whether you want sets of three or six different patterns, then make into coasters as explained above.

11 To make the holder for the set of coasters, take the remaining timber and cut a 4–6mm (¼in) section from the bottom.

If you do not have the facilities to do this yourself, your local builders' merchants or wood yard will probably oblige. Stick this piece back to the bottom – using double-sided sticky tape – ready for stack cutting.

12 Use compasses to draw template 16B for the coaster-holder onto the top of the timber, again using the template as a guide for the radius of the two circles. Alternatively, the template can be stuck directly on to the timber if preferred.

13 Cut around the outside circle of the template then separate the two pieces.

14 Taking the largest top section only, drill a pilot hole in the middle, then cut round the inner circle using a scrollsaw or fretsaw. Glue this onto the base and leave to dry.

15 To facilitate removing the coasters from the holder, cut out a section from the side of the holder measuring 35mm (1⅜in) deep by 15mm (⅝in) wide, and round it at the bottom, as shown.

16 If liked, the top of the holder can also be rounded over to give a smooth finish. Varnish in the same way as the coasters (see stage 9) then, once the varnish is dry, place the coasters in the holder.

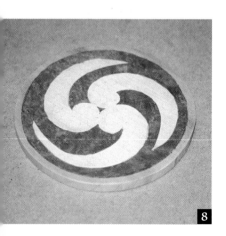

TRIVET

he knotwork featured in this project shows how a circular pattern can be incorporated into a design. The circle was important to the Celts, not only because it is a solar symbol, but also because the unending line is a reminder of the continuous circle of life.

Going back much further in time, it was the shape adopted for the construction of many megalithic sites, Stonehenge being perhaps one of the most famous circles of all. Early huts were round, as were hill forts, because the circle was thought to be protective both physically and spiritually.

The knotwork design for the trivet is made up of two bands, one which weaves its way around the design without any knots, and a second much busier band that has all the work to do, looping back on itself all the way around. An alternative way to highlight the knotwork bands is to paint them in two different colours with diluted emulsion paint before varnishing.

The feet of the trivet are similar to a lion decoration from *The Book of Kells*. He seemed such a humble and subservient creature, I thought he deserved a bit of recognition, even though I have put him in a position of further subservience.

Lion decoration in the style of
The Book of Kells

Traditionally, the lion represents strength and majesty, and in Celtic art it is the evangelist symbol for St Mark (although in *The Book of Durrow* it was used as a symbol for St John). The lion was sometimes given wings to emphasise its divine nature.

Method

1 Use spray adhesive to stick the trivet template, 17C, to the larger of the two pieces of timber or you can, if you prefer, trace the design onto the surface using carbon paper between the template and timber.

2 Cut round the outside of the design using a scrollsaw or hand fretsaw. If necessary, cut in at right angles to the points where the knotwork will weave, to be sure of a sharp outline.

3 If not already done at step 1, peel off the design and transfer it to the face of the timber as described.

4 Rout out the circle to hold the cork coaster. Make this the depth of the thickness of the coaster, plus 2mm (³⁄₃₂in) to allow for the depth of the knotwork carving. You can use chisels and gouges for this, if a router is not available.

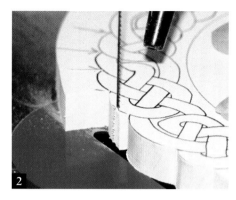
2

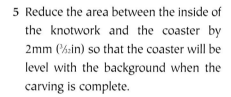

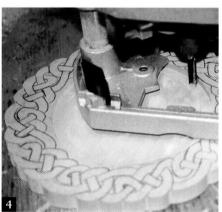
4

5 Reduce the area between the inside of the knotwork and the coaster by 2mm (³⁄₃₂in) so that the coaster will be level with the background when the carving is complete.

6 Reduce the small triangles between the knotwork to a depth of 2mm (³⁄₃₂in). I found a sharp chip knife most suitable for this.

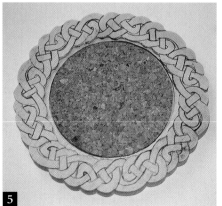
5

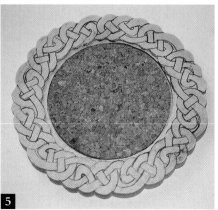
6

Materials

Photocopies of templates 17A, 17B and 17C on page 114

Timber measuring approx. 160 x 160 x 10mm (6¼ x 6¼ x ³⁄₈in) (beech)

Timber measuring approx. 200 x 70 x 25mm (8 x 2¾ x 1in) (lime)

Cork coaster, 95mm (3¾in) in diameter

Repositionable spray adhesive

Heatproof polyurethane varnish (clear)

Emulsion paints (optional)

Tools

Scrollsaw or fretsaw

Router (optional)

Chisels and gouges

Chip knife or craft knife

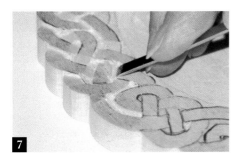

7 Score along the lines that cross the knotwork then, working at right angles, reduce the timber down towards the cut to give the appearance of weaving under. Repeat the process for all the crossing points.

8 Glue the coaster in place in the centre rebate.

9 Make a card template of the lion motif 17A and use it to draw three lion shapes.

10 Cut out each lion on a scrollsaw or fretsaw, then cut out the small areas under the chin and behind the tail.

11 Transfer the designs onto both sides of each lion, either by copying freehand, or tracing from the template.

12 Draw the following lines on the front edge of each lion: down the centre of the back legs; 8mm ($^5/_{16}$in) in from the edge of each front paw; 5mm ($^3/_{16}$in) in from each side of the forehead; and 8mm ($^5/_{16}$in) in from each side of the snout, as shown.

13 Score along these lines, and along the lines of the design on both sides of each lion. Reduce the material around the end of the tail on the lion's right side to make it stand out, then carve out the waste between the tail and the back leg, curving the edges as you

work. Carve the tail inwards to make it appear to come from behind the legs. Slope the end of the back leg so that it tucks in behind the front paw. Round the sides of the back and front legs and paws.

14 Reduce the material around the base of the tail on the lion's left side, and carve a 'V' between the back leg and chest, curving them inwards. Make the tail appear to weave behind the legs by sloping it inwards. Slope the end of the back leg as on the left side, to tuck it behind the front paw. Round over the legs and paws.

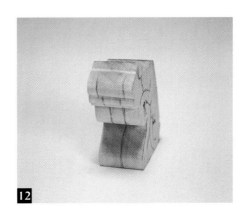

Progressive stages of carving each side of the lion

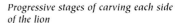

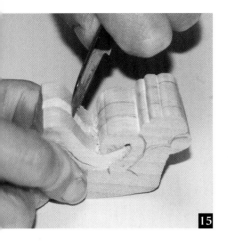

15

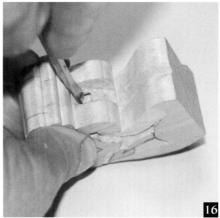

16

17

15 On the front edge cut a 'V' between the back legs along the scored line, and round over the edges.

16 Cut out the space between the front paws, cutting it right back until it meets the area that has previously been cut under the chin, in step 10. Round over the sides of the paws.

17 Narrow the head from each side up to the scored lines and round the edges, leaving the mane full width.

18 Shape the back and shoulders but leave the top flat, as this is where the trivet will be fastened. Dip the chest in below the arms and shape the mane and face. If any sanding is necessary, sand before finally adding the eye, nose and mouth.

19 Glue the three lions to the underside of the trivet, placing them equal distances apart (120°), so that the edge of the trivet is touching the mane. Place a weight on the trivet until the glue has firmly set.

20 Varnish the trivet and lions with two or three coats of clear polyurethane.

18

CLADDAGH MIRROR

he Claddagh motto is 'In love, in friendship, let us reign'. A little of the history of the Claddagh design has been referred to in the Claddagh Lovespoon project (page 20), now I'll explain more about its creator, Richard Joyce.

Richard Joyce had been taken captive in the Mediterranean by Algerian pirates and sold to a Moorish goldsmith, who trained him in metalwork and set him to work. When William III became king of England in 1689 he secured the release of all his subjects held captive by the Moors. Richard Joyce's master tried to persuade him to stay by offering his daughter's hand in marriage, but Joyce preferred to return to his native fishing village,

Claddagh, near Galway in Ireland. Here he set up his own business making jewellery, and designed the Claddagh ring. The rings became immensely popular and were passed as family heirlooms from mother to daughter.

The design of the Claddagh ring became known across the world as emigrants left Ireland at the time the great famine of 1847–49. Many more rings were left as security back in Ireland, and used to raise the fare to escape the famine; poignantly, many were never reclaimed.

One variation that sometimes appears in the design is the height of the crown: a high-domed crown would have been worn by a queen and a low-domed crown belonged to a king.

Materials

Photocopies of templates 18A, 18B and 18C on pages 115–117, enlarged by 142%

Carbon paper

Timber measuring 380 x 360 x 30mm (15 x 14¼ x 1³⁄₁₆in) (sycamore)

4mm plywood, 320 x 320mm (12⅝ x 12⅝in)

Mirror, diameter 305mm (12in)

Clear varnish

Glazier's points or tacks

Picture rings and wire

Tools

Scrollsaw, jigsaw or fretsaw

Router (optional)

Rotary multi-tool (optional)

Selection of woodcarving tools

Chip knife or craft knife

In this project the Claddagh design forms part of the frame, which is reminiscent of the ring shape. An eternal knot weaves around the border.

Method

1 Photocopy the three templates of the design and cut along the dotted lines. Tape them together to form the complete design, making sure that the places where the actual design meets are firmly joined and taped.

2 Cut the design out, including the small gaps between the hands, heart and crown, and then trace the template shape onto the face of the timber, using carbon paper.

3 The mirror frame can now be cut out. You can do this with a scrollsaw, jigsaw or fretsaw but, if you have access to a router, a far more accurate part-circle can be made. If you wish to use a router, first locate the centre of the circle on your timber. The diagrams below show you how to do this accurately.

4 Apply glue to the centre base of the timber, attach it firmly to a piece of scrap wood, then either clamp the base to the worktop, or use a routing mat to hold it in place.

5 Attach a trammel bar to the router and locate the pin in the centre mark. Cut round the circle as far as the cuffs of the Claddagh design, making several passes, each 3–4mm (³⁄₁₆in) deeper than the last, until the full cut is made.

6 Reset the router to cut the inner circle, again cutting as far as the cuffs of the Claddagh design.

At this stage, whilst the router is still set up for face cutting, the two fine lines on each side of the knotwork can be incised, using a 2mm (³⁄₃₂in) straight router bit, to a depth of 2.5m (¹⁄₈in). Routing gives a very even line and makes the knotwork carving easier, but this step is optional, as the lines can be carved using a chip-carving knife and gouge at step 12.

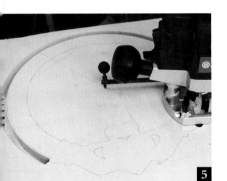

5

6

How to find the centre of a circle

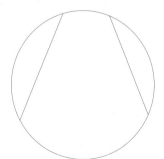

Draw two lines on the inside of the circle as shown

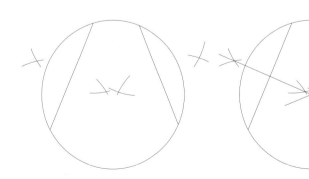

Set the compasses at just over half the length of the lines. Place the point at one end and mark inside and outside the line. Repeat on the other line

Draw a line between the two sets of crosses. The centre of the circle is at the point where these two lines cross

7 Cut out the small gaps between the hands, heart and crown and then turn the work over (so that the back is uppermost), in order to mark the position for the mirror rebate.

8 Lay the mirror on the back of the frame so that the gaps between hands, heart and crown are covered – this will leave it off-centre, towards the bottom.

9 Draw round the mirror and then find the centre of this circle, as described previously.

10 Rout a deep rebate for the mirror inside the line, to a depth of 15mm (¾in), i.e. half the depth of the frame. There is no need to rout the centre of the circle, as this will be removed when the remaining Claddagh design is cut out.

11 Cut out the remaining section of the frame, the Claddagh design, using a scrollsaw, fretsaw or jigsaw.

12 On the front of the frame, draw in the line where the cuffs meet the frame. Using a straight chisel, bevel the frame down to about 2–3mm (⅛in) below the level of the cuff on each side of the frame.

13 Transfer the knotwork design onto the frame using carbon paper and reduce the background around the knotwork by 3mm (⅛in). This will be easier if the two guiding bands were routed at stage 6. The outside edges of the knotwork can be removed by cutting down vertically with a small chisel or gouge and then lifting the waste out.

14 The small areas between the tight bends can be removed with the sharp point of a knife.

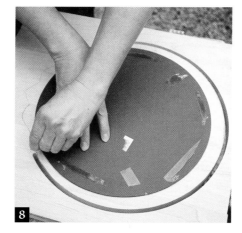

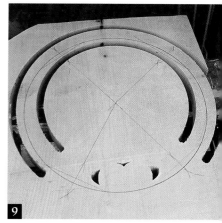

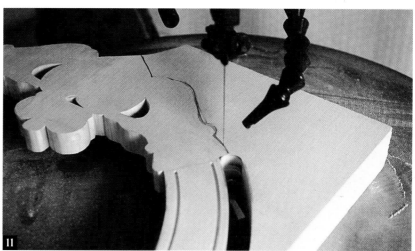

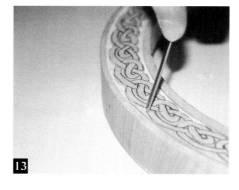

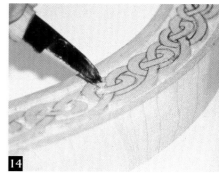

the same time, round it over top and bottom to get rid of the squared-off look. Shape the hands by reducing the depth and angling the fingers downwards.

17 Curve the sides of the heart down to meet the fingers at the sides. Round the thumbs and make a dip at the base of the thumb. Use your own hands, or those of a willing friend, to see the shape they make in this position.

15 When all the background has been removed, score all the crossing lines and lower each side to give the effect of interweaving.

16 When shaping the Claddagh part of the design, it is advisable to do the basic shaping of one half first as a guide, then you can shape the other side to match it. Carve the crown after the hands and heart have been completed.

Begin by angling the cuff down in towards the roll at the wrist, and matching the slope on the other side, from the hand to the roll. Take it down quite deep to give good definition. At

18 Curve the edges of the roll at the wrist and round over the bottom edges of the hand. Shape the top of the heart, curving it in below the bottom edges of the crown.

19 Carve the other side of the design to match and, when it is completely even and balanced, sand it smooth.

Next, draw in the lines for the fingers and frills on the cuffs. The dark mark on the fingers in the photo is from a knot that I thought I would just miss – I was wrong. That's wood for you. It does, however, serve as a useful reminder that you should take note of knots and cracks when choosing timber for a project.

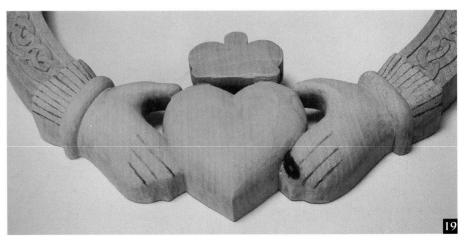

20 Score along the lines, then cut a deep, steep-sided groove in between the fingers. Round over the sides of the fingers, then shape the frills of the cuffs in a similar way, although the grooves are not made as deep.

21 To shape the crown, first reduce the depth by 2–3mm (⅛in) overall, so that it does not appear as high above the heart. Transfer the design onto the crown and score along the straight horizontal line.

22 Round over the edges of the straight section, top and bottom.

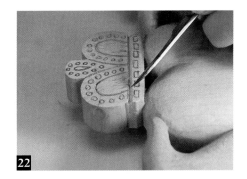

23 Score along the two arched lines and then slope the pattern down by about 2mm (⅛in) to leave the 'padded cushions' on the crown raised at the bottom.

24 Re-draw the lines and, at the top of the arches, bevel the cushions inwards to give a soft, rounded appearance. Cut some creases at the bottom of the cushions and round over the bottom edge.

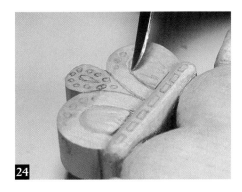

25 Slope in the bottom of the teardrop shape at the top of the crown and carve out the little shape in the middle by 1mm (¹⁄₁₆in).

26 Decorate the arches of the crown using a punch. I actually decorated mine using an old posidrive screwdriver, but a round punch could be used.

27 Cut a backing piece for the mirror from the 4mm (⁵⁄₃₂in) plywood. Draw round the mirror to get the correct size.

28 Since the frame is made from a single piece of timber, the grain will run in all directions round it. To minimise any movement of the wood, coat the frame with at least two coats of varnish, to ensure a really good seal – this will also help prevent the mirror being cracked by movement in the wood.

29 Place the mirror in the rebate with the plywood backing behind. Fasten it in place using glazier's points or tacks.

30 Screw two small picture rings into the back of the frame, level with each other on either side of the ring, and thread a piece of picture wire through to hang the mirror.

Stained Glass Uplighter

*A window of the ambulatory,
St Oswald's Church, Ashton*

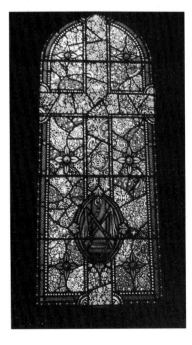

Occasionally one comes across a hidden sanctuary in the most unexpected place, as I did when I visited a church at Ashton-in-Makerfield, near Wigan, Lancashire, to view the Harry Clarke stained glass windows. I was prepared to be in awe of the windows themselves, having already seen some of his work, but I was taken by surprise to find such an oasis of calm just a short distance from a roaring motorway.

For anyone who is not familiar with the name of Harry Clarke, he was undoubtedly one of the twentieth century's greatest stained glass artists, with a skill and vision rarely encountered in this medium. Unfortunately, the very nature of stained glass means that few people have the opportunity to see it in all its splendour unless they are able to visit the churches, and photographic reproduction is rarely able to do justice to his jewel-like colours and stunning designs (see left).

As a small tribute to Harry Clarke, I have included a painted glass panel in this uplighter. The uplighter is designed to hang on a wall and gives off a soft light which makes the panel glow like a stained glass window. The front is removable to allow access to the light fitting and it has a carved zoomorphic design at the base.

ARRY CLARKE WAS BORN IN DUBLIN, IRELAND IN 1889, THE SON OF AN ENGLISH father and an Irish mother.

His work was strongly influenced by the work of Aubrey Beardsley, as can be seen in his illustrations for the literary works of authors such as Edgar Allan Poe, Samuel Taylor Coleridge, W. B. Yeats, Alexander Pope and Hans Christian Andersen.

His reputation as a stained glass artist was firmly established through his first major commission, to design and make the windows of the Honan Chapel in Cork, Ireland.

Although he suffered ill health for most of his short life, he produced a vast amount of work for churches not only in Ireland, but also in England, Scotland, Wales, Australia and New Jersey, USA.

His early work in stained glass was executed entirely by himself but, as demand increased and his health deteriorated, his studio undertook more of the work, but always under his supervision and to his high standards.

Harry Clarke died in Switzerland in 1931, at the age of 41, having succumbed to the tuberculosis that he had battled with for so long.

St Oswald's Church, Ashton-in-Makerfield

The seven windows of St Oswald's Church, Ashton-in-Makerfield, Lancashire

Materials

Photocopies of templates 19A and 19B, on pages 118–19, both enlarged by 133%, and of 19C on page 120

MDF measuring: 300 x 355 x 9mm ($11^{13}/_{16}$ x 14 x $^{11}/_{32}$in) – main front section

282 x 70 x 9mm ($11^1/_4$ x $2^3/_4$ x $^{11}/_{32}$in) – small front section

130 x 272 x 9mm ($5^1/_8$ x $10^{11}/_{16}$ x $^{11}/_{32}$in) – 2 pieces, for sides

405 x 300 x 6mm ($15^{15}/_{16}$ x $11^{13}/_{16}$ x $^1/_4$in) – back

124 x 282 x 12mm ($4^7/_8$ x $11^1/_4$ x $^1/_2$in) – base

Continued overleaf

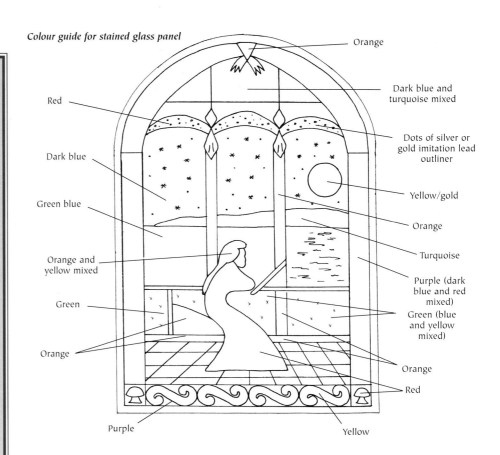

Colour guide for stained glass panel

- Orange
- Red
- Dark blue
- Green blue
- Orange and yellow mixed
- Green
- Orange
- Purple
- Dark blue and turquoise mixed
- Dots of silver or gold imitation lead outliner
- Yellow/gold
- Orange
- Turquoise
- Purple (dark blue and red mixed)
- Green (blue and yellow mixed)
- Orange
- Red
- Yellow

Materials continued

Timber measuring 210 x 50 x 10mm (8¼ x 2 x ⅜in) for carving (lime)

Clear acrylic sheet measuring 290 x 200mm (11⁷⁄₁₆ x 8in)

3mm self-adhesive lead strip

Tube of silver imitation lead outliner

Glass paints in dark blue, turquoise, red, orange, yellow/gold, green

Wood glue

Countersunk screws

2 magnetic catches with flat metal plates

All-purpose glue

Strip light fitting, 265mm (10⁷⁄₁₆in) long, with 211mm (8⁵⁄₁₆in), 30w light tube, mains fitting

Acrylic primer

White paint

Metallic blue enamel paint (or colour of your choice)

Tools

Scrollsaw, jigsaw or fretsaw

Drill

Router (optional)

Carving tools

Method for the lightbox

1 Begin by making the painted stained glass panel, as this will be used to get an accurate frame for the front of the uplighter. Take the clear acrylic sheet and tape template 19A underneath so the design shows through from below. Cut round the outside of the design using a scrollsaw at slow speed, or use a fretsaw. A slow cutting speed is necessary to avoid melting the plastic as it is being cut, which might jam the blade.

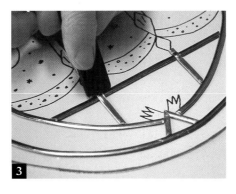

3

2 Clean the face of the acrylic sheet, and then lay strips of self-adhesive lead along the lines of the design showing through from underneath, peeling off the lead-backing as you go. If you are using the type of lead that comes in a double strip, cut it along the middle first, using ordinary household scissors.

3 Following the manufacturer's instructions, use the tool supplied with the lead strip to press it down on the sheet and seal the edges, making sure no gaps are left for the paint to seep through.

4 The small lines of the face, scrolls, the diamond shapes at the top, etc. are drawn on using the imitation lead outliner directly from the tube.

5 When the outliner is dry, fill in the design with the glass paints, using this colour chart as a guide.

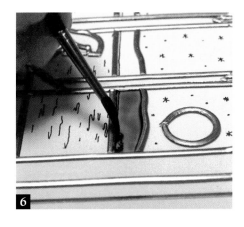

6 To make the hills look moonlit, paint in a line of dark blue at the bottom whilst the turquoise is still wet. Allow it to blend in.

7 When the sea has been painted, but before it is completely dry, etch out the lines of the waves using a wooden toothpick, or round end of a small paintbrush. The lines will show through as a silvery light when lit up. Do the same for the stars in the sky.

8 Once the glass paint is completely dry, use scissors to cut away the surplus area around the outer edge of the template, beyond the outside edge of the lead. Don't worry if the panel outline changed when the lead strip was applied – it may well end up slightly different from the original line of the template – as it will provide you with a very accurate template to use in the next stage.

9 Cut the timber for the main front piece to the size indicated in the materials list. Place the template you have just re-sized on the timber, pattern side up, positioning it about 60mm (2⅜in) from each side and top, and about 30mm (1¾₆in) from the bottom. Draw round the template, and then make the top

arch shape by marking off points 60mm (2⅜in) away from the drawn line all the way round to where it meets the sides. Join up the various points, to form the arch and cut around this shape.

10 Drill a pilot hole inside the previous line you drew, for the scrollsaw (or fretsaw) blade to pass through, then cut out the template shape. Offer up the painted panel to the frame, to check that the opening is the correct size before proceeding. Make a rebate in the back of the frame – the same depth as the acrylic sheet – for the stained glass panel to fit in. Draw round the panel to get the right shape for the rebate.

11 Cut the two side panels using template 19B (on page 119).

12 Cut the smaller lower front panel to the size indicated in the materials list, and then angle the top edge down towards the back to match the angle created by the notch on the two sidepieces. This can be done using a plane or sander.

13 Mark the back piece to the size given in the materials list, use the front as a template to create the same arch shape at the top, then cut it out.

14 Drill two holes in the back near the top, which will be used to hang the light on the wall. Use a drill bit large enough for a screw head to pass through, and then drill a smaller hole above it to create an upside down keyhole shape that the screw will rest on.

15 Cut the base to size and cut out a small square at the back to allow the light cable to pass down.

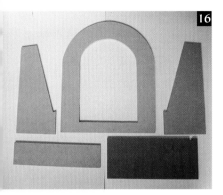

16 This photograph shows all the components of the light box, except for the back, which is longer than the front and without the hole.

17 Paint the inside of all the pieces white, which will help show off the stained glass when the light is not on.

18 When dry, assemble as follows, countersinking all the screw heads: screw the strip light fitting onto the base, placing it centrally along the length; glue and screw the smaller front piece to the front of the base. Glue and screw the sides to the base and short front piece. Glue and screw the back to the base and sides, ensuring that the light cable fits down the hole between the base and the back.

19 Screw the metal plate for the magnetic catch to the inside of each side, approximately 70mm (2¾in) down from the top. Screw the other part of the catch to the inside of the front piece to match up with the metal plate. This will hold the front securely in place, but enable it to be removed, for access to the light.

20 Check that all the joins are lightproof, particularly where the main front piece rests on the sloping part of the small, lower front piece. (If you have difficulty with this, you can glue a strip of felt behind the join to stop any light escaping, after it has all been painted.

21 Paint the box as desired. I used four coats of metallic blue enamel paint to give a deep richness to the box.

22 When the paint is dry, glue the painted panel into place in the rebate. If there are any gaps showing between the outer lead decoration and the frame, use the imitation lead to fill them in so that no stray light will show when it is lit up.

Method for the carving

i Transfer the template for the carving (19C on page 120) onto the remaining piece of timber. Cut out the internal shaded areas and then cut round the outside, using a scrollsaw or fretsaw.

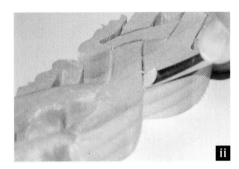

ii Score the lines of the design and then reduce the wood where the design appears to weave under another band.

iii Round over the sides of the bodies and legs, and shape the claws as for the eagle plaque and zoomorphic lovespoon (see pages 26 and 61).

iv Shape the heads by reducing around the forehead and cheeks, and then rounding off the edges. Reduce the teeth by about 1mm below the jaw and round them over.

v Glue the dog motif onto the front panel.

vi Finally, hook the uplighter over two wall screws.

The completed dog motif

BATHROOM SET

Materials

Photocopies of templates
20A–20I, on pages 121–25.
Enlarge 20F by 111%

Timber measuring
145 x 1100 x 18mm
(5¾ x 43 x ¾in) (pine)

Timber measuring
300 x 240 x 18mm
(11¾ x 9½ x ¾in) (pine)

Timber measuring 800 x
50 x 4mm (31½ x 2 x ⁵⁄₃₂in)
(American hard maple)

Wood glue

10 x wood screws,
countersunk

6 x cross-slot chipboard
screws, countersunk

6 x plastic screw covers

1 x 100mm nail (4in)

Sprung toilet-roll holder

Glass or plastic tumbler,
approx. 56mm (2¼in)
diameter at base

Wood primer

Emulsion or gloss paint in
two contrasting shades

Clear varnish

This final project is made up of three bathroom fittings – toothbrush holder, towel ring and toilet roll holder – which are decorated with fish and mermaid motifs.

Fish appear on Celtic metalwork such as coins and cauldrons, and on many Pictish stone carvings, particularly in the form of a salmon. In Celtic mythology the salmon represents knowledge and wisdom. In Irish mythology, a particular Boyne River salmon was said to be empowered with great wisdom and whoever was first to eat its flesh would gain great knowledge and have the power to foretell future events. When Finnegas the bard caught it, he gave it to his apprentice Finn McCool to cook, with strict instructions not to taste the flesh. As the fish was cooking, Finn prodded it with his thumb and burnt himself. He instinctively put the thumb into his mouth and unwittingly became the possessor of the great knowledge. He went on to become a great leader, and legend has it that every time he faced a difficult decision, or wanted to see into the future, he would suck his thumb to call upon his magic powers.

In Celtic mythology, female deities were associated with fresh water, and natural springs and wells were often believed to have healing powers.

The image of the mermaid as half-woman, half-fish appears in *The Book of Kells*, along with a merman. The mermaid in this project is based on a carving on one of the Meigle Stones housed in the Meigle Museum in Angus, Scotland. She appears on a small fragment of architectural frieze, between two animals.

With the coming of Christianity, the fish became a symbol of Christ.

Method

1 Make copies of templates 20A–20F, paste them onto thin card and cut them out.

Take templates 20A (back plate for the toilet roll holder) and 20B (the back plate for both the toothbrush holder and towel ring); draw around these onto the 145mm (5¾in) wide timber, making two copies of template 20B, one for each item. Cut the shapes out of the timber using a scrollsaw or fretsaw.

Draw around templates 20C (the arms of the toilet roll holder), 20D

(the arms of the towel ring) and 20E (the toothbrush holder) onto the remaining 145mm (5¾in) wide timber. Cut out the shapes, using a scrollsaw or fretsaw.

2 If you have a router, rout a decorative edge on the face of the three back plates and the arms of the toilet roll holder and towel ring holder. I used a 6mm (¼in) diameter ovolo bit. If you don't have access to a router, the edges can be rounded over using a sanding drum attached to a Dremel or other rotary tool, or by using a medium (120) grade sandpaper.

3 Mark the position of the rebates on the face of the three back plates and arms of the toilet roll holder. This can be done either by drawing around the outside guidelines of templates 20G, 20H and 20I, or by cutting the shape out of the card template and drawing round the cutout.

Rout the rebates to a depth of 4mm (⁵⁄₃₂in). If you do not have a router, score around the outline with a sharp knife and remove the inside waste using a chisel. See the three photos of the assembled parts, on page 86.

Tools

Scrollsaw, or jigsaw and fretsaw

Drill and screwdriver

Router (optional) or sandpaper

Carving tools

3

4 Cut pieces 20C and 20D in half down the centre line, where marked on the templates.

5 On the remaining piece of 18mm (¾in) timber, draw a circle approximately 222mm (8¾in) in diameter, then draw another circle 18mm (¾in) inside that. Use template 20F to give the top shape of the ring where indicated by the template. (If necessary, erase the dotted line to avoid confusion when cutting out.)

Cut the piece out, using a scrollsaw or fretsaw. If you have a router, you could use it to get an accurate shape for the part-circle, following the instructions for the Claddagh Mirror on page 71.

6 Round over the front and rear faces of the ring, using a router if available. If not, the corners can be sanded off, leaving the ring in a more squared-off shape. Keep the two ends of the top extension square, where it will sit between the two arms.

7 Drill a hole lengthwise through the top of the piece as shown, making it slightly larger in diameter than the nail.

8 Cut the head and point off the nail to leave it 77mm (3in) long. This can be done using a cut-off disc in a rotary tool, or a hacksaw.

9 Drill a hole at the centre of each inside face of the towel ring arm pieces, template 20D, to a depth of 6mm (¼in).

10 Cut out the five holes, for the tooth mug and toothbrushes, where shown on template 20E.

11 Using a countersink bit in the drill, make a depression on the inside of each toilet roll holder arm (template 20C). Position the depressions 35mm (1⅜in) from the front of the arms.

12 Drill pilot holes through the back plates of the toilet roll holder, toothbrush holder and towel ring, to allow them to be screwed to the wall when finished. Position the holes near the top, on either side of the rebate.

13 To make the decorative inserts, cut the 4mm (⁵⁄₃₂in) thick timber roughly to the length of the motifs; you will need two of template 20G, four of

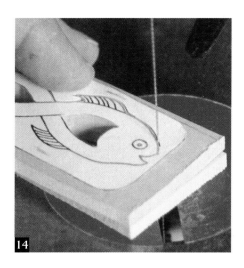
14

17

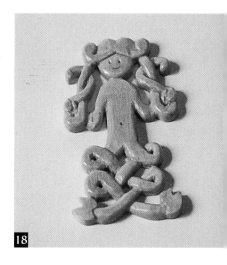
18

template 20H, and three of template 20I. Stack the timber together for each motif using double-sided sticky tape, as described for the Celtic Knotwork Border on page 13.

14 Place the appropriate motif on top of each stack and drill pilot holes to make the internal cuts. Cut out the internal waste areas and then cut round the outside of the motif.

15 To make the two fish (template 20G), carefully separate the pieces and transfer the lines of the design onto opposite faces of the timber, so that each fish faces in the opposite direction.

16 Score along the lines and reduce either side of the crossing bands. Reduce the depth of the fins on the body and tail. Round over the sides of the bands and head, and mark in the eye. Use a small chisel to score lines on the fins.

17 To make the four mermaids, first make the internal cuts, and use a small 2mm (³⁄₃₂in) drill bit to make the holes in the tight curls of the legs.

18 Cut round the outside of the design and carefully separate the pieces. Transfer the lines onto each face, and then carve in the usual way.

19 Make three copies of template 20I, in the same way.

20 Seal the carved decorative pieces with a clear varnish.

21 Prime and paint the back plates of the remaining pieces – toilet roll holder, toothbrush holder and towel ring – and the arms and towel ring itself, using a darker contrasting colour in the rebated areas. Paint the face of the six screw-head covers to match the back plates. If you prefer the natural look of the wood, the set can be varnished instead, in which case use a contrasting dark varnish for the rebates.

22 To assemble the set, screw the arms of the toilet roll holder onto the back plate from behind, leaving a distance of 123mm (4⁷⁄₈in) between them. Place the sprung holder in between, locating it in the countersunk holes.

16

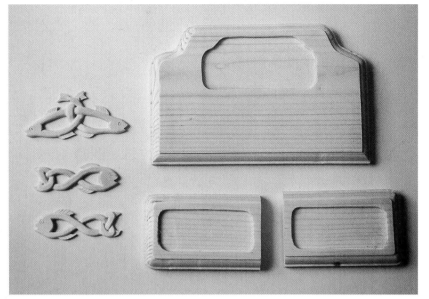

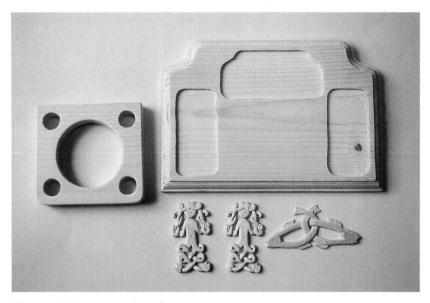

The assembled components for each part of the set

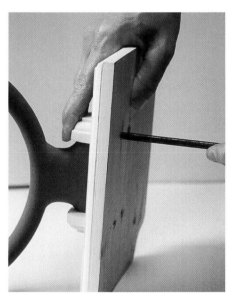

Screw the toothbrush holder onto the back plate from behind.

Pass the cut-down nail through the top of the towel ring before placing an arm on each end of the nail, then screw the arms in place on the remaining back plate. The towel ring should then swing out freely on its mount.

Glue all the decorative pieces in place, positioning the two fish motifs

– facing forward – on the outside of each arm of the toilet roll holder, the three fish motifs at the top of each back plate, and the four mermaids at each side of tooth mug holder and towel ring.

23 Screw each piece to the bathroom wall through the pre-drilled holes, using the cross-slot screws. Press a painted screw cover over each screw head.

The project designs

he designs needed to make all the projects in this book are included here, and they should be photocopied or traced off. Unless otherwise stated, the designs are drawn to the correct size to make the projects. Where a template needs to be enlarged when photocopying, the size of enlargement is given.

Areas that are to be cut out inside the designs are shown in diagonal shading on the designs. (Not all the step-by-step photographs show this shading.)

Areas that need clarifying for any other reason – for example where background has to be reduced but not completely removed – are indicated by vertical shading.

Celtic knotwork border *See page 12*

1 A

This template needs to be enlarged by 125%

Knotwork overlays *See page 15*

2A

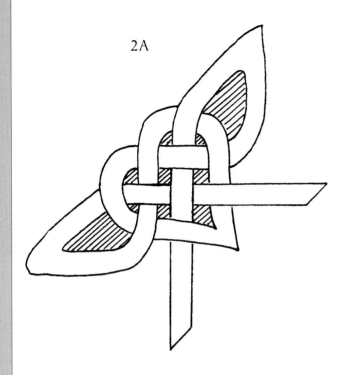

2B

2C

2D

Initial memo holder *See page 18*

3A

This template needs to be enlarged by 125%

3B

This template needs to be enlarged by125%

Initial memo holder *See page 18*

3C

This template needs to be enlarged by 125%

Initial memo holder *See page 18*

3D

This template needs to be enlarged by 125%

Initial memo holder *See page 18*

3E

This template needs to be enlarged by 125%

Claddagh lovespoon *See page 20*

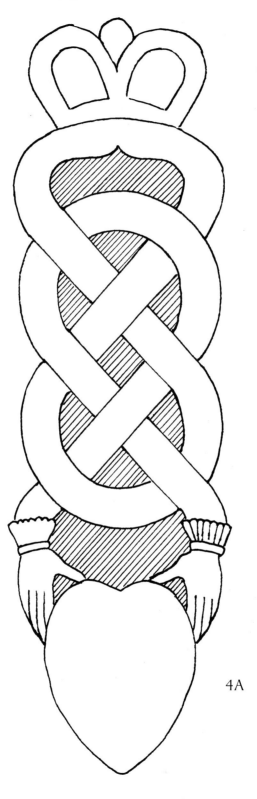

4A

This template needs to be enlarged by 111%

Double photo frame *See page 23*

5A

Eagle wall plaque *See page 26*

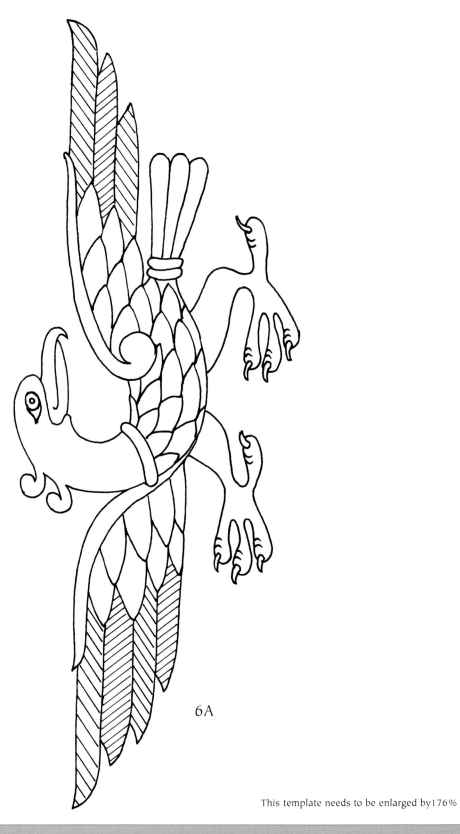

6A

This template needs to be enlarged by176%

Message board *See page 31*

7A

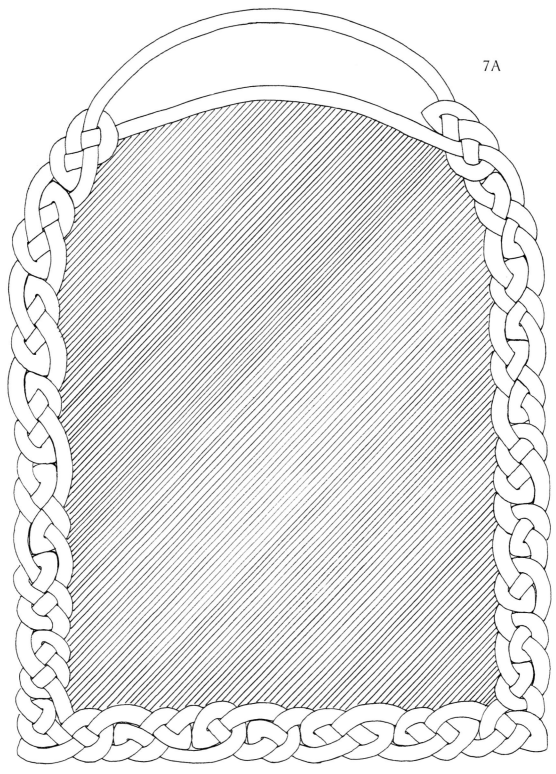

This template needs to be enlarged by 188%

Message board   *See page 31*

7B

7C

7D

'Tree of Life' seed keeper *See page 34*

8A

This template needs to be enlarged by 125%

'Tree of Life' seed keeper *See page 34*

8B

This template needs to be enlarged by 125%

'Tree of Life' seed keeper *See page 34*

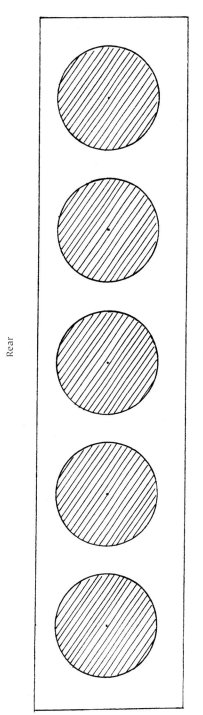

Rear

Front

8C

This template needs to be enlarged by 125%

Hand mirror *See page 37*

Do not cut out shaded areas

9A

This template needs to be enlarged by 125%

Dragon trinket box *See page 41*

10A

Template for brass insert

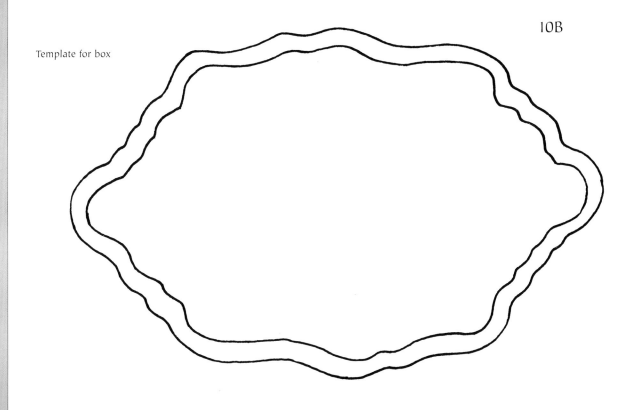

10B

Template for box

Knotwork jigsaw boxes *See page 44*

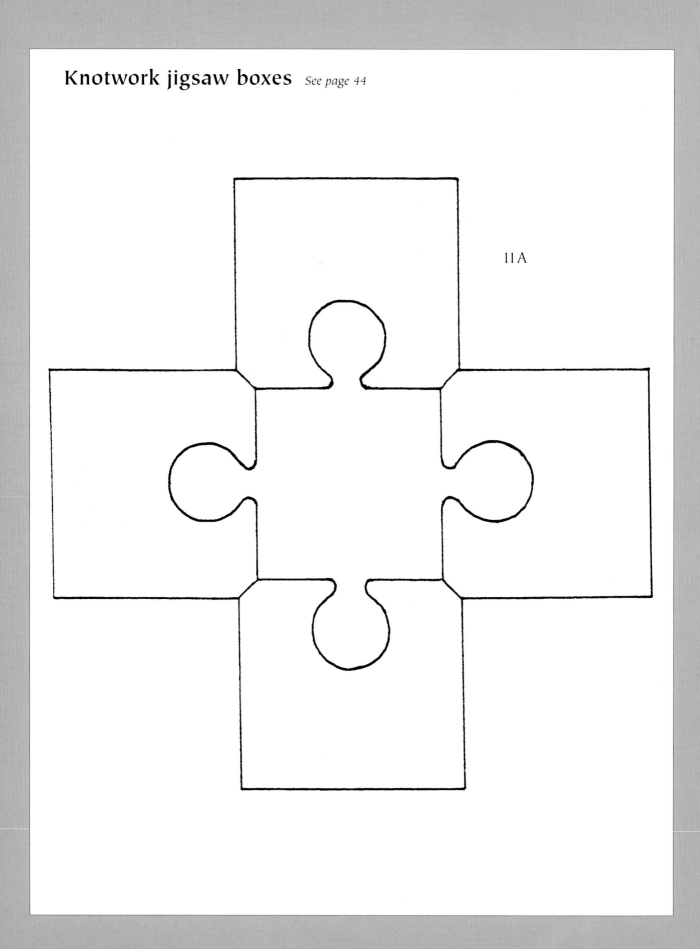

11A

Knotwork jigsaw boxes *See page 44*

11B

Knotwork jigsaw boxes *See page 44*

IIC

Celtic cross *See page 48*

12A

This template needs to be enlarged by 125%

Fun photo frame *See page 52*

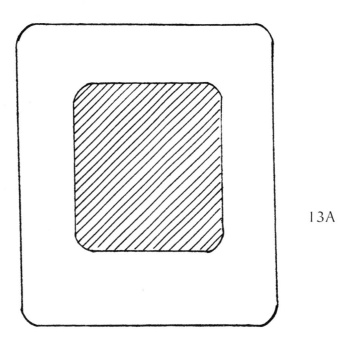

13A

13B

13C

Mirrored candle sconce *See page 57*

14B Sides

Zoomorphic lovespoon *See page 61*

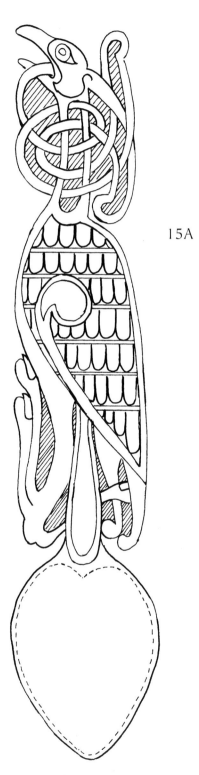

15A

This template needs to be enlarged by 125%

Coasters in holder *See page 64*

Template for coasters

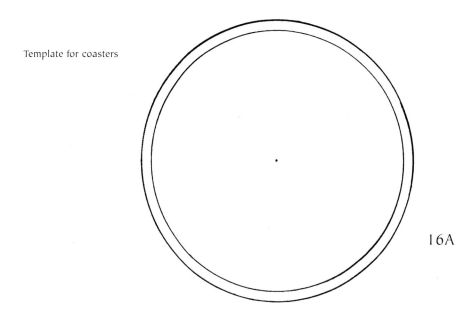

16A

Template for holder

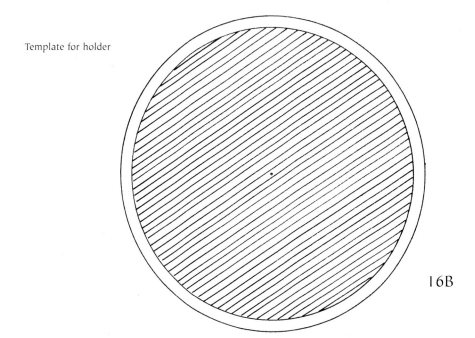

16B

These templates need to be enlarged by125%

Coasters in holder *See page 64*

16C

16D

16E

16F

16G

16H

These templates need to be enlarged by 125%

Trivet   *See page 67*

17A

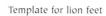

Template for lion feet

17B

17C

Template for trivet

These templates need to be enlarged by125%

Claddagh mirror *See page 71*

18A

Templates 18A, B and C to be joined

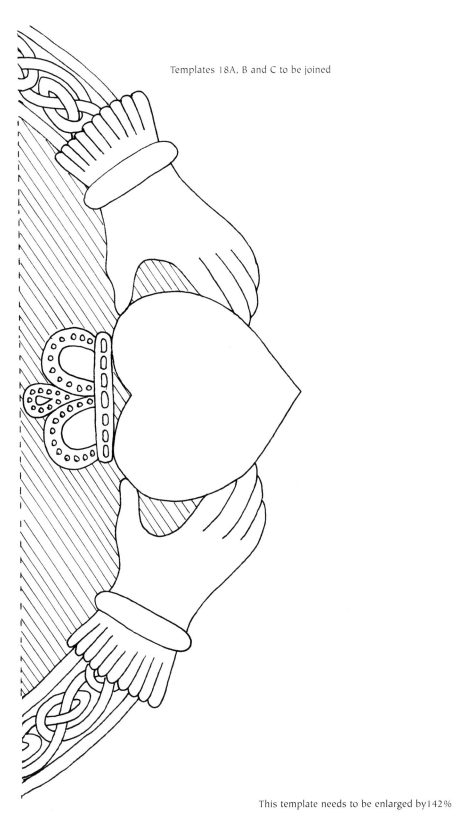

This template needs to be enlarged by 142%

Claddagh mirror *See page 71*

18B

This template needs to be enlarged by 142%

Claddagh mirror *See page 71*

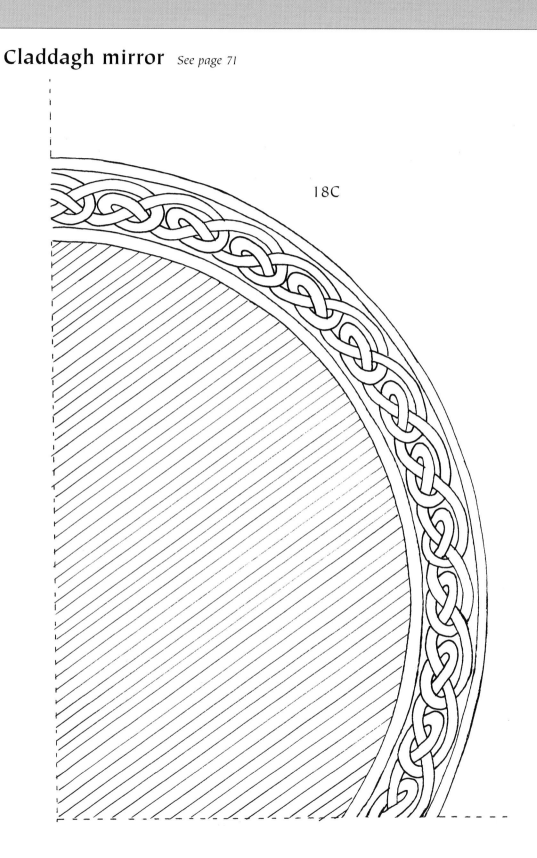

18C

This template needs to be enlarged by 142%

Uplighter *See page 76*

See page 76

Template for stained glass panel

19A

This template needs to be enlarged by 133%

Uplighter *See page 76*

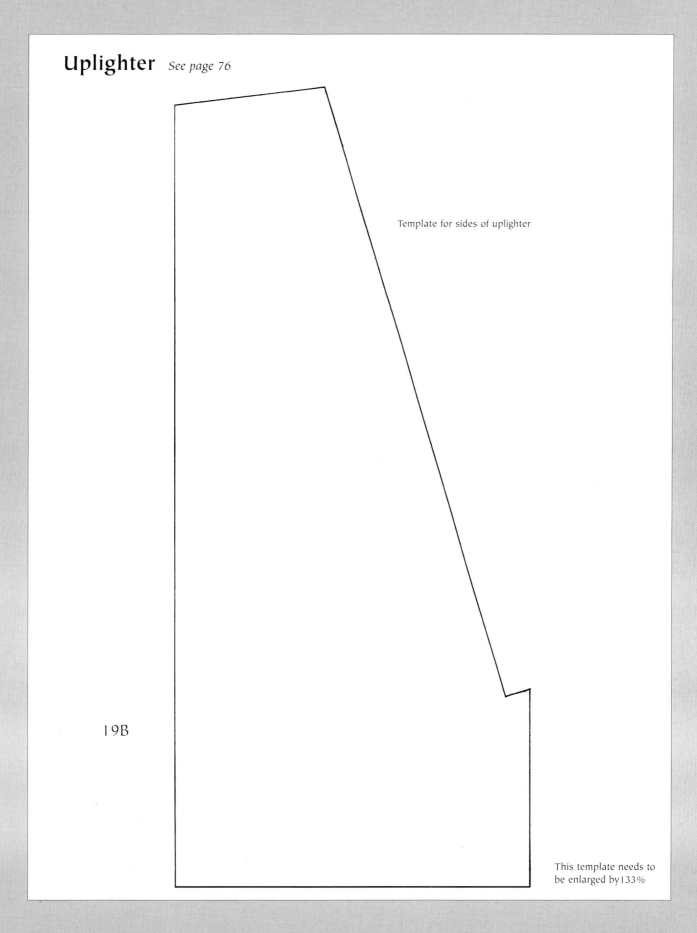

Template for sides of uplighter

19B

This template needs to be enlarged by133%

Uplighter *See page 76*

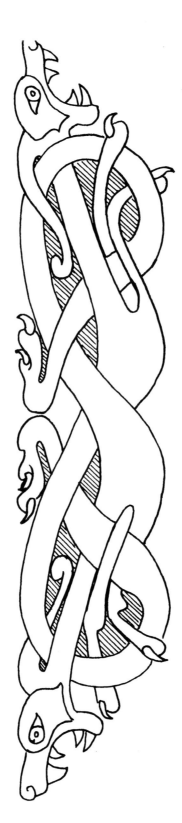

Template for carving on front of uplighter

19C

Bathroom set *See page 82*

Template 1 – cut one

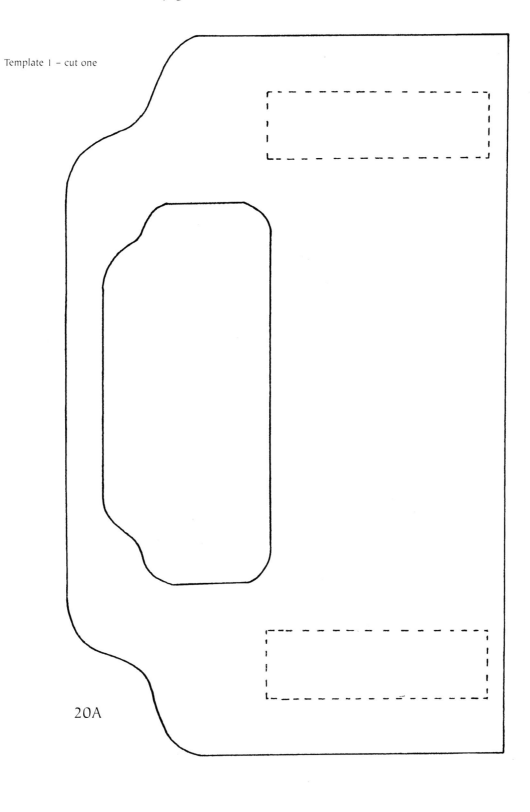

20A

Bathroom set *See page 82*

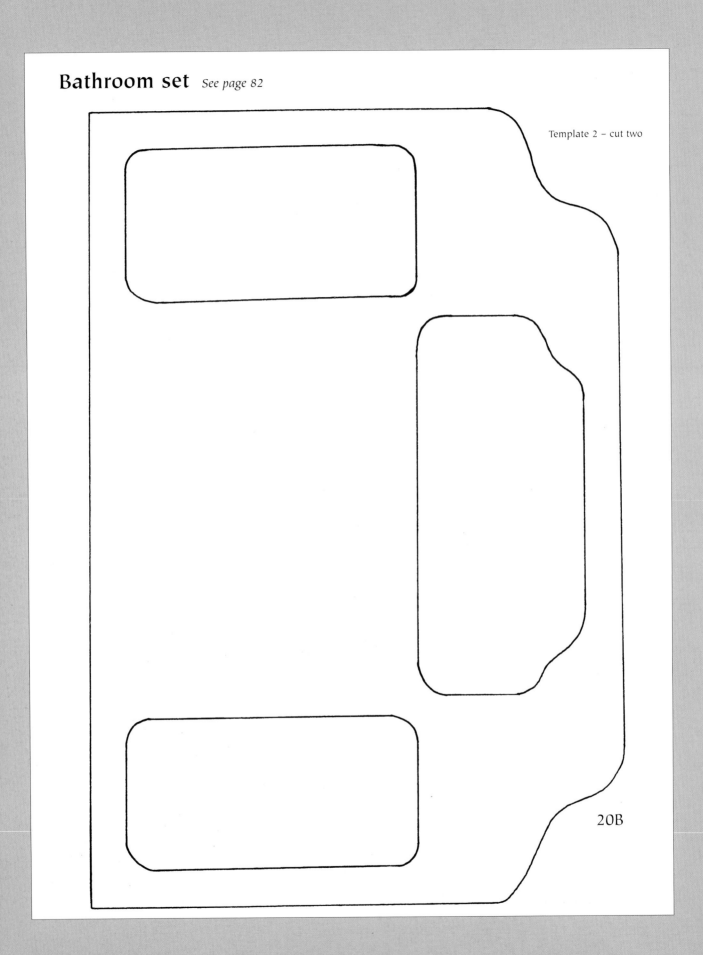

Template 2 – cut two

20B

Bathroom set *See page 82*

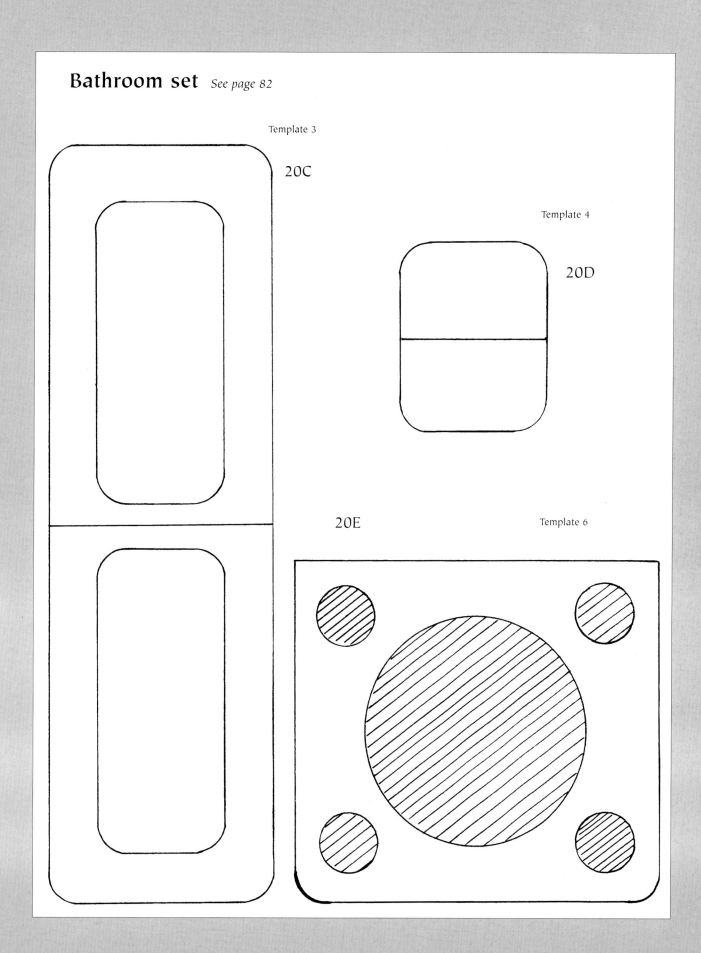

Template 3

20C

Template 4

20D

20E

Template 6

Bathroom set *See page 82*

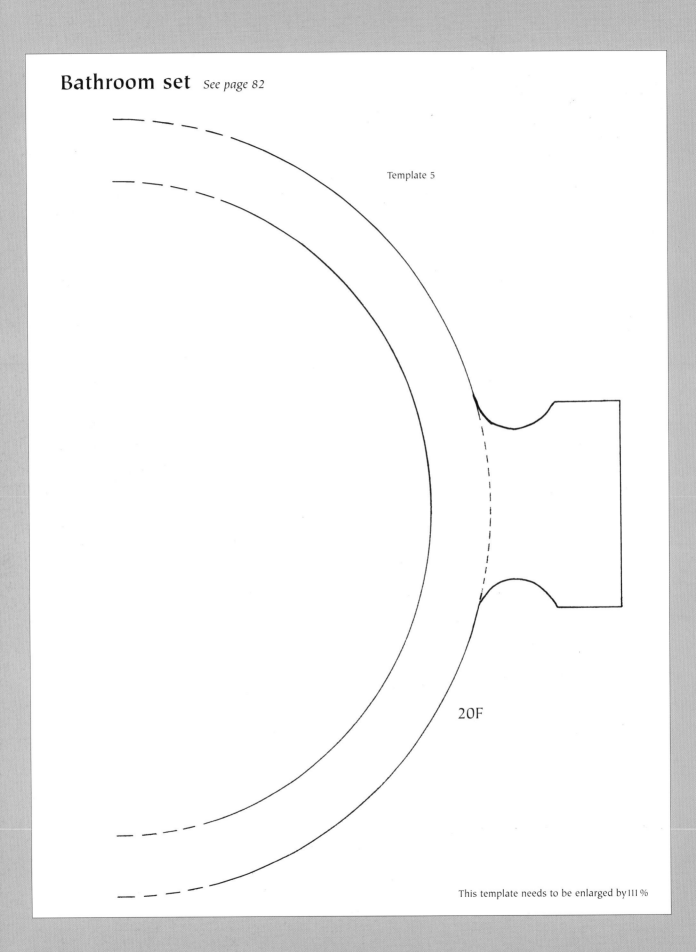

Template 5

20F

This template needs to be enlarged by 111 %

Bathroom set *See page 82*

20H

Template 7   20G

Template 9

20I

Template 8

Glossary

Ancestor stones
Flat pebbles, incised or painted, found in a cave in the French Pyrenees, which were believed to contain the spirits of the dead.

Anthropomorphic
Designs based upon the form of humans

Book shrine
A box made of metal, or wood and metal, in which a gospel book was stored for protection.

Carpet page
An ornamental page in a gospel book that consists purely of decoration, with no text.

Folio
One page of a manuscript book.

Insular
Produced in Britain or Ireland as opposed to Continental Europe.

La Tène
Prehistory period, named after a Swiss archaeological site.

Megalithic
Made of or marked by the use of big stones.

Phyllomorphic
Design based upon the form of leaves and plants.

Recto
The front of a folio.

Repoussé
Relief design on metalwork produced by hammering from behind.

Triskele
Three-legged spiral motif.

Verso
The back of a folio.

Votive
Given in fulfilment of a vow.

Zoomorphic
Design based upon the forms of animals, birds and reptiles.

Further reading

This list includes the titles of some books on related subjects for further study, a selection of books on Celtic art and design and a CD Rom.

Bain, George
Celtic Art. The Methods of Construction
(Constable, 1951)

Balchin, Judy
Celtic Glass Painting
(Search Press, 2000)

Bowe, Nicola Gordon
The Life and Work of Harry Clarke
(Irish Academic Press, 1989)

Crawford, H. S.
Irish Carved Ornament
(Mercier Press, 1980)

Davis, Courtney
The Celtic Art Source Book
(Blandford, 1988)

Meehan, Aidan
Animal Patterns
(Thames & Hudson, 1992)

Meehan, Bernard
The Book of Kells
(Thames & Hudson, 1994)

Meehan, Bernard
The Book of Durrow
(Town House Dublin, 1996)

Pennick, Nigel,
The Celtic Cross
(Blandford, 1997)

Ritchie, Anna
Picts
(Historic Scotland, 1999)

Sturrock, Sheila
Celtic Knotwork Designs
(GMC Publications, 1997)

Sullivan, Sir Edward
The Book of Kells
(Studio Editions, 1986)

Wood, Juliette
The Celts
(Duncan Baird Publishers, 1998)

Zaczek, Iain
The Chronicles of the Celts
(Collins & Brown, 1996)

Zaczek, Iain
The Art of the Celts
(Parkgate Books, 1997)

Wallace, Patrick F.
A Guide to the National Museum of Ireland
(Town House Dublin, 2000)

CD Rom, *The Book of Kells*
Editor, Bill Simpson
(Trinity College Library Dublin, 2000)

About the author

Glenda Bennett was born and educated in Kent. She moved to the north of England in the early 1970s, but has also lived in Sarawak, Japan and the south west of Ireland.

Glenda is self-taught in her art and craft skills, and has received several commissions. These include watercolour paintings for greetings cards, pen and ink artwork for tea towels of English villages and the artwork for commemorative Millennium pottery for the Pendle Tourist Information Office.

Glenda studied calligraphy with the East Lancashire Guild of Calligraphers, which furthered her interest in Celtic art. This in turn led to her studying and devising methods of turning drawn Celtic designs into woodcarvings.

Glenda lives in Lancashire with her partner, and is mum to two children and their partners, and a stepdaughter.

Index

Page numbers in **bold** refer to illustrations

TITLES AVAILABLE FROM
GMC Publications
BOOKS

WOODCARVING

Beginning Woodcarving — GMC Publications
Carving Architectural Detail in Wood: The Classical Tradition — Frederick Wilbur
Carving Birds & Beasts — GMC Publications
Carving the Human Figure: Studies in Wood and Stone — Dick Onians
Carving Nature: Wildlife Studies in Wood — Frank Fox-Wilson
Carving on Turning — Chris Pye
Celtic Carved Lovespoons: 30 Patterns — Sharon Littley & Clive Griffin
Decorative Woodcarving (New Edition) — Jeremy Williams
Elements of Woodcarving — Chris Pye
Essential Woodcarving Techniques — Dick Onians
Lettercarving in Wood: A Practical Course — Chris Pye
Relief Carving in Wood: A Practical Introduction — Chris Pye
Woodcarving for Beginners — GMC Publications
Woodcarving Tools, Materials & Equipment (New Edition in 2 vols.) — Chris Pye

WOODTURNING

Bowl Turning Techniques Masterclass — Tony Boase
Chris Child's Projects for Woodturners — Chris Child
Contemporary Turned Wood: New Perspectives in a Rich Tradition — Ray Leier, Jan Peters & Kevin Wallace
Decorating Turned Wood: The Maker's Eye — Liz & Michael O'Donnell
Green Woodwork — Mike Abbott
Intermediate Woodturning Projects — GMC Publications
Keith Rowley's Woodturning Projects — Keith Rowley
Making Screw Threads in Wood — Fred Holder
Turned Boxes: 50 Designs — Chris Stott
Turning Green Wood — Michael O'Donnell
Turning Pens and Pencils — Kip Christensen & Rex Burningham
Woodturning: A Foundation Course (New Edition) — Keith Rowley
Woodturning: A Fresh Approach — Robert Chapman
Woodturning: An Individual Approach — Dave Regester
Woodturning: A Source Book of Shapes — John Hunnex
Woodturning Masterclass — Tony Boase
Woodturning Techniques — GMC Publications

WOODWORKING

Beginning Picture Marquetry — Lawrence Threadgold
Celtic Carved Lovespoons: 30 Patterns — Sharon Littley & Clive Griffin
Celtic Woodcraft — Glenda Bennett
Complete Woodfinishing (Revised Edition) — Ian Hosker
David Charlesworth's Furniture-Making Techniques — David Charlesworth
David Charlesworth's Furniture-Making Techniques – Volume 2 — David Charlesworth
Furniture-Making Projects for the Wood Craftsman — GMC Publications
Furniture-Making Techniques for the Wood Craftsman — GMC Publications

Furniture Projects with the Router — Kevin Ley
Furniture Restoration (Practical Crafts) — Kevin Jan Bonner
Furniture Restoration: A Professional at Work — John Lloyd
Furniture Restoration and Repair for Beginners — Kevin Jan Bonner
Furniture Restoration Workshop — Kevin Jan Bonner
Green Woodwork — Mike Abbott
Intarsia: 30 Patterns for the Scrollsaw — John Everett
Kevin Ley's Furniture Projects — Kevin Ley
Making Chairs and Tables – Volume 2 — GMC Publications
Making Classic English Furniture — Paul Richardson
Making Heirloom Boxes — Peter Lloyd
Making Screw Threads in Wood — Fred Holder
Making Woodwork Aids and Devices — Robert Wearing
Mastering the Router — Ron Fox
Pine Furniture Projects for the Home — Dave Mackenzie
Router Magic: Jigs, Fixtures and Tricks to Unleash your Router's Full Potential — Bill Hylton
Router Projects for the Home — GMC Publications
Router Tips & Techniques — Robert Wearing
Routing: A Workshop Handbook — Anthony Bailey
Routing for Beginners — Anthony Bailey
Sharpening: The Complete Guide — Jim Kingshott
Space-Saving Furniture Projects — Dave Mackenzie
Stickmaking: A Complete Course — Andrew Jones & Clive George
Stickmaking Handbook — Andrew Jones & Clive George
Storage Projects for the Router — GMC Publications
Veneering: A Complete Course — Ian Hosker
Veneering Handbook — Ian Hosker
Woodworking Techniques and Projects — Anthony Bailey
Woodworking with the Router: Professional Router Techniques any Woodworker can Use — Bill Hylton & Fred Matlack

UPHOLSTERY

Upholstery: A Complete Course (Revised Edition) — David James
Upholstery Restoration — David James
Upholstery Techniques & Projects — David James
Upholstery Tips and Hints — David James

TOYMAKING

Scrollsaw Toy Projects — Ivor Carlyle
Scrollsaw Toys for All Ages — Ivor Carlyle

DOLLS' HOUSES AND MINIATURES

1/12 Scale Character Figures for the Dolls' House — James Carrington
Americana in 1/12 Scale: 50 Authentic Projects — Joanne Ogreenc & Mary Lou Santovec
The Authentic Georgian Dolls' House — Brian Long

CRAFTS

GARDENING

PHOTOGRAPHY

Close-Up on Insects	*Robert Thompson*
Double Vision	*Chris Weston & Nigel Hicks*
An Essential Guide to Bird Photography	*Steve Young*
Field Guide to Bird Photography	*Steve Young*
Field Guide to Landscape Photography	*Peter Watson*
How to Photograph Pets	*Nick Ridley*
In my Mind's Eye: Seeing in Black and White	*Charlie Waite*
Life in the Wild: A Photographer's Year	*Andy Rouse*
Light in the Landscape: A Photographer's Year	*Peter Watson*
Outdoor Photography Portfolio	*GMC Publications*
Photographing Fungi in the Field	*George McCarthy*
Photography for the Naturalist	*Mark Lucock*
Professional Landscape and Environmental Photography: From 35mm to Large Format	*Mark Lucock*
Rangefinder	*Roger Hicks & Frances Schultz*
Viewpoints from *Outdoor Photography*	*GMC Publications*
Where and How to Photograph Wildlife	*Peter Evans*

ART TECHNIQUES

Oil Paintings from your Garden: A Guide for Beginners	*Rachel Shirley*

VIDEOS

Drop-in and Pinstuffed Seats	*David James*	Twists and Advanced Turning	*Dennis White*
Stuffover Upholstery	*David James*	Sharpening the Professional Way	*Jim Kingshott*
Elliptical Turning	*David Springett*	Sharpening Turning & Carving Tools	*Jim Kingshott*
Woodturning Wizardry	*David Springett*	Bowl Turning	*John Jordan*
Turning Between Centres: The Basics	*Dennis White*	Hollow Turning	*John Jordan*
Turning Bowls	*Dennis White*	Woodturning: A Foundation Course	*Keith Rowley*
Boxes, Goblets and Screw Threads	*Dennis White*	Carving a Figure: The Female Form	*Ray Gonzalez*
Novelties and Projects	*Dennis White*	The Router: A Beginner's Guide	*Alan Goodsell*
Classic Profiles	*Dennis White*	The Scroll Saw: A Beginner's Guide	*John Burke*

MAGAZINES

WOODTURNING ◆ WOODCARVING ◆ FURNITURE & CABINETMAKING

THE ROUTER ◆ NEW WOODWORKING ◆ THE DOLLS' HOUSE MAGAZINE

OUTDOOR PHOTOGRAPHY ◆ BLACK & WHITE PHOTOGRAPHY

TRAVEL PHOTOGRAPHY

MACHINE KNITTING NEWS ◆ BUSINESSMATTERS

The above represents a full list of all titles currently published or scheduled to be published.
All are available direct from the Publishers or through bookshops, newsagents and specialist retailers.
To place an order, or to obtain a complete catalogue, contact:

GMC Publications,
166 High Street, Lewes, East Sussex BN7 1XU, United Kingdom
Tel: 01273 488005 Fax: 01273 402866
E-mail: pubs@thegmcgroup.com

Orders by credit card are accepted

JUL 2003